Cambridge Elements

Elements in the History of Philosophy and Theology in the West
edited by
Alexander J. B. Hampton
University of Toronto

IRIS MURDOCH AND THE TRANSCENDENT

Charles Taliaferro
St. Olaf College

Jil Evans
Independent Scholar and American Artist

Shaftesbury Road, Cambridge CB2 8EA, United Kingdom

One Liberty Plaza, 20th Floor, New York, NY 10006, USA

477 Williamstown Road, Port Melbourne, VIC 3207, Australia

314–321, 3rd Floor, Plot 3, Splendor Forum, Jasola District Centre, New Delhi – 110025, India

103 Penang Road, #05–06/07, Visioncrest Commercial, Singapore 238467

Cambridge University Press is part of Cambridge University Press & Assessment, a department of the University of Cambridge.

We share the University's mission to contribute to society through the pursuit of education, learning and research at the highest international levels of excellence.

www.cambridge.org
Information on this title: www.cambridge.org/9781009631594
DOI: 10.1017/9781009631600

© Charles Taliaferro and Jil Evans 2026

This publication is in copyright. Subject to statutory exception and to the provisions of relevant collective licensing agreements, no reproduction of any part may take place without the written permission of Cambridge University Press & Assessment.

When citing this work, please include a reference to the DOI 10.1017/9781009631600

First published 2026

A catalogue record for this publication is available from the British Library

A Cataloging-in-Publication data record for this Element is available from the Library of Congress

ISBN 978-1-009-63157-0 Hardback
ISBN 978-1-009-63159-4 Paperback
ISSN 3033-3954 (online)
ISSN 3033-3946 (print)

Cambridge University Press & Assessment has no responsibility for the persistence or accuracy of URLs for external or third-party internet websites referred to in this publication and does not guarantee that any content on such websites is, or will remain, accurate or appropriate.

For EU product safety concerns, contact us at Calle de José Abascal, 56, 1°, 28003 Madrid, Spain, or email eugpsr@cambridge.org

Iris Murdoch and the Transcendent

Elements in the History of Philosophy and Theology in the West

DOI: 10.1017/9781009631600
First published online: February 2026

Charles Taliaferro
St. Olaf College

Jil Evans
Independent Scholar and American Artist

Author for correspondence: Charles Taliaferro, taliafer@stolaf.edu;
Jil Evans, Jilevans216@gmail.com

Abstract: Iris Murdoch challenged the intellectual climate of her day. She transcended the reductive, behavioristic view of consciousness, sought to transcend the theory of values that focuses on will and desire, and defended instead a transcendent understanding of goodness and the Good that can transform us, leading us to renounce our egocentric nature. Her positive view of individual freedom and value led her to oppose strict gender roles and structuralism. Murdoch proposed that, ideally, our lives may be a pilgrimage toward the Good. She believed that the experience of beauty and art can enhance the pursuit of the Good. And yet Murdoch shunned the quest to discover some meaningful, transcendent reality (God or an impersonal, purposive force) to understand ourselves and the cosmos. In her words, "we are simply here." The authors ask whether Murdoch's foregoing a search for a broader transcendent reality to understand why we are here is compelling.

Keywords: goodness, consciousness, Platonism, beauty, art

© Charles Taliaferro and Jil Evans 2026

ISBNs: 9781009631570 (HB), 9781009631594 (PB), 9781009631600 (OC)
ISSNs: 3033-3954 (online), 3033-3946 (print)

Contents

	Preface	1
1	Iris Murdoch In Situ	2
2	The Importance of Being Conscious	13
3	The Transcendent, Transformative Power of Goodness	23
4	Beauty, Truth, and Good Art	35
5	Transcendence and the Natural World	48
	Bibliography	68

Preface

It is fall of 1991, and I am sitting on a sloping bank of the Cherwell River in University Parks, Oxford, England. Hunched over a small canvas, I am concentrating on capturing in oil paint the moving reflections of low-hanging beech and chestnut tree branches, clouds, and broken spikes of sunlight, when I feel a presence nearby. I turn to look up over my shoulder, where a woman in a long, checkered wool overcoat and bucket hat is standing a few yards away.

"It's very difficult, isn't it?" she says.

"Yes," I reply, grateful for the acknowledgment and somewhat disheartened that my efforts are not more impressive. I turn to look back at the river, and a few moments later, Iris Murdoch resumes her walk.

Murdoch was well-acquainted with painting. She painted during her student days, taught in the Royal College of Art, seriously considered becoming an art historian, and paid homage to paintings in some of her novels. She brought the power of images to all her work. Her critical analysis of philosophical positions was made alive through images and pictures. Her exploration of the aesthetic dimension of philosophical reasoning was a significant creative layer and guide in her apprehension of moral values and human consciousness. Her contributions brought a new vitality to philosophical thinking, addressing our problems in life as it is lived. "Philosophers are artists, and metaphysical ideas are aesthetic; they are intended to clarify and connect, and they certainly satisfy deep emotional needs" (Murdoch, 1993: 37).

For Murdoch, our activity of thinking with language has imagery "riddled" with the sensible (Murdoch, 1997: 39). Metaphor is involved all the time in our everyday search to make connections with our experiences. "Metaphor is not a peripheral excrescence upon the linguistic structure, it is its living centre" (1997: 40).

Murdoch understood one of philosophy's tasks "involves seeing the absolute oddity of what is familiar and trying to formulate really probing questions about it" (1997: 8). Analogous to poetry, philosophy involves "a difficult purification of one's statements, of thought emerging in language" (1997: 5). Her own work demonstrates an unwavering commitment to attending to difficult questions and the deep pleasures that emerge in doing so.

Jil Evans

I have been surprised by Iris Murdoch in three ways.

First, I have come to realize how ingenious Murdoch's work was in challenging the philosophy of mind of her day. Postwar British philosophy was antagonistic to recognizing the robust reality of inner subjective experience. As coauthor Jil Evans and I argue in Section 2, Murdoch challenged the then-dominant quasi-behaviorism long before well-known philosophers like Thomas Nagel did. The history of modern philosophy of mind needs to recognize Murdoch's timely, significant contributions.

Second, over many years of writing and teaching about the role of Platonism in early modern philosophy, I have connected Murdoch's Platonism with the seventeenth-century Cambridge Platonists. Like Murdoch, the Cambridge Platonists argued for moral realism and gave a central role to love in their value theory and metaphysics; they opposed reductive materialism and determinism. Seeing Murdoch's work in this historical perspective impacted my understanding of the history of philosophy and religion.[1]

Third, while the focus of *Murdoch and the Transcendent* is Murdoch's philosophical work, her success as a novelist led me to adjust my teaching philosophy. In many classes I invite students to write, in addition to formal academic essays, philosophically interesting fiction.

Charles Taliaferro

1 Iris Murdoch In Situ

> The truth-seeking mind is magnetized by an Independent multiform reality.
> Iris Murdoch (1993: 301)

Iris Murdoch is an ideal subject for this series of Cambridge Elements – the history of philosophy and theology in the West – given her respect for theology and her substantial contributions to philosophy. "Philosophy and theology, for all their persistent mutual hostilities, have always maintained relations and, contrary to some appearances, still do" (1993: 229). Murdoch's philosophical work and her successful career, authoring twenty-six novels, several plays, and a volume of poetry, present us with the challenge of addressing a large body of work that extends in many directions. As George Steiner observed: "Murdoch's papers, lectures, reviews are like a light-house: the beam circles around and around the central axis of the Good taking in, at each successive sweep, a vast and diverse horizon" (1997: xii). Our task requires us to survey the complex intellectual climate in which she wrote in order to bring the boldness of her contributions into context and relief. She opposed the reigning philosophical methodologies and arguments of her day.

---

[1] Taliaferro, "The Sovereignty of the Good in Seventeenth-Century Philosophy," *Evidence and Faith*, 11–109.

In this section we offer a sketch of her life, describe some of the main philosophical forces active in her day, and introduce her proposed alternative to the status quo. Future sections will be more detailed and evaluative of what we see as compelling and enduring in Murdoch's work. While we reference some of her novels, limitations of space compel us to focus on her philosophical and theological work.

1.1 The Truth-Seeking Mind

Jean Iris Murdoch (1919–1999) was born in Dublin, Ireland, to Anglo-Irish parents who moved to London in her early years. An only child, she grew up as an Anglican and there is some evidence that, despite her subsequent atheism and rejection of traditional Christianity, she had a lifelong respect for Christian teachings about love, forgiveness, repentance, and redemption, as well as its "mythology" and rites, especially prayer and meditation. She wrote, "We do not need to believe in God to make sense of the motto of Oxford University: *Dominus illuminatio mea*" (1997: 425). The motto "The Lord is my light" is taken from Psalm 27. Her assertion suggests that she retained some notion of the divine or the sacred, what she would call the Good or goodness, and the importance of people being illuminated and transformed by goodness. Murdoch wrote so extensively on God, Christianity, and religion that her husband, John Bayley, referred to her as a theologian.[2]

Later in life she came to have a growing attraction to Buddhism. She appreciated the shared Buddhist and Christian commitment to compassion and opposition to selfishness. While she sometimes described herself as a Buddhist Christian, it is implausible to think of her as fully subscribing either to Buddhism or to traditional Christianity.[3]

From 1938 to 1942 at Somerville College, Oxford University, Murdoch undertook the course of Literae Humaniores (otherwise known as "Greats"), which included classics, ancient history, and philosophy. Among her influential tutors were Donald M. MacKinnon, a philosophical theologian and devout Anglican, and Eduard Fraenkel, a Jewish classics scholar who fled Nazi Germany in 1934. While at Somerville, she was attracted to Marxism and was a member of the Communist Party during those student years (approximately 1938–1942).

After graduating from Oxford with first-class honors, she spent five years working for the British Treasury and the United Nations Relief and Rehabilitation Administration, serving in London, Belgium, and Austria.

---

[2] Baley, "Foreword," *Iris Murdoch: A Life*, xi.
[3] Robjant, "As a Buddhist Christian; the misappropriation of Iris Murdoch," 993–1008.

We have recently been given a fuller portrait of Murdoch during these years through her letters and diary from 1939 to 1945 in *Iris Murdoch, A Writer at War*, edited by Peter J. Conradi. These personal papers provide an intimate look at Murdoch's transition from her student days as a member of a performing troupe, the Magpie Players, to being part of the British war effort and caring for refugees and displaced persons. We see Murdoch's growing passion to be a writer. In a letter dated July 1943, she wrote, "Later on in August I hope to spend a week in Oxford where I shall not walk at all but shall think the whole time. What about? My chief thought will probably be 'Whether or not I am a writer' – a thought that has obsessed me."[4] Her letters to two wartime friends – Frank Thomson, poet and British commando officer, and David Hicks, serving the British Council overseas – reveal close observations of the people in her life, some of whom she loved passionately.

In 1947 she spent a year as a postgraduate, studying philosophy at Newnham College, Cambridge University, where she met philosopher Ludwig Wittgenstein. Despite his formidable reputation, Murdoch had reservations about Wittgenstein's philosophical methodology and his view about the meaning of language.

Murdoch returned to Oxford in 1948 as a tutor at St. Anne's College, lecturing in philosophy. She retired from St. Anne's as Honorary Fellow in 1963 and turned to writing full-time, except for three years of occasional teaching at the Royal College of Art.

From Murdoch's undergraduate days at Oxford onward, she formed close, lifelong friendships with three women – Elizabeth Anscombe, Philippa Foot, and Mary Midgley – who all went on to become prominent philosophers. They shared and revered the same tutor, Donald M. MacKinnon, who stood out in his opposition to the fascism of Franco in the Spanish Civil War (opposing Britain's policy of being noninterventionist) and for his commitment to metaphysics, ethics, and religious faith in the face of skepticism by other Oxford dons and students. Murdoch, Anscombe, Foot, and Midgley challenged the dominant, predominantly male Oxford philosophers. This cohort has recently been celebrated by two books: *Metaphysical Animals: How Four Women Brought Philosophy Back to Life*, by Clare Mac Cumhaill and Rachael Wiseman, and *The Women Are Up to Something: How Elizabeth Anscombe, Philippa Foot, Mary Midgley, and Iris Murdoch Revolutionized Ethics*, by Benjamin J. B. Lipscomb. Both books highlight how Murdoch and her friends renewed

---

[4] Conradi (ed.), *Iris Murdoch, A Writer at War*, 150.

the practice of philosophy, making room for engaging in the philosophy of love, focusing on substantial moral concerns involving interior reflection, and insisting on the importance of metaphysics.

Consider Midgley's account of how she, Murdoch, and other women found a different way of practicing philosophy than the way of their male peers.

> As a survivor of the wartime group, I can only say: sorry, but the reason was indeed that there were fewer men about then.... What is wrong is a particular style of philosophising that results from encouraging a lot of clever young men to compete in winning arguments. These people then quickly build up a set of games out of simple oppositions and elaborate on them until, in the end, nobody else can see what they are talking about.... By contrast, in the wartime classes – which were small – men (conscientious objectors, etc.) were present as well as women, but they weren't keen on arguing.
>
> It was clear that we were all more interested in understanding this deeply puzzling world than putting each other down. That was how Elizabeth Anscombe, Philippa Foot, Iris Murdoch, Mary Warnock and I, in our various ways, all came to think out alternatives to the brash, unreal style of philosophising – based essentially on logical positivism – that was current at the time.[5]

Another female philosopher, not based in Oxford, should be added to those who challenged male philosophical hegemony and had an important influence on Murdoch: Simone Weil. She stressed the vital role of perception and attention in apprehending values. She fought in the Spanish Civil War and was part of the French Resistance, dying in 1943 in England. Murdoch was fascinated by Weil's reflections on politics and culture, as well as her philosophical journey from Platonism to a mystical form of Christianity. She called Weil's *The Need for Roots* "one of the very few profound and original political treatises of our time."[6]

After the war, many Oxford philosophers had an ambivalent, sometimes hostile view of Continental philosophers (Heidegger, Sartre, Camus, and Beauvoir). Murdoch did not share this aversion. She met Sartre in 1945. Her first book was *Sartre: Romantic Rationalist*, published in 1953. The book begins with addressing Sartre's novels, perhaps providing a clue that Murdoch herself would later turn to writing novels, for their potential literary and philosophical power. While Murdoch praises Sartre as a playwright, she is highly critical of his philosophy of freedom and values.

---

[5] Midgley, "The Golden Age of Female Philosophy."
[6] Conradi, *The Saint and the Artist*, 16.

She describes his "obsessive and hypnotic world picture" (Murdoch, 1987: 10) as consisting of a dialectic between freedom (free consciousness) and the given world of other people, history, and traditions. The "en-soi," that which is unfree, must be overcome heroically by the individual alone. Sartre's phrase "hell is other people," from his play *No Exit*, led Murdoch to conclude: "There is no suggestion in Sartre's account that love is connected with action and day to day living; that it is other than a battle between two hypnotists in a closed room" (1987: 130–131). Her positive views of Sartre are rarely without qualification. "What Sartre certainly has given is a brilliant and generally instructive self-analysis. We are tempted to say to him: this is one kind of person, yes: but there are others" (1987: 127). Still, Murdoch presented Sartre as a philosopher who deserves serious attention. "His philosophy is not just a piece of irresponsible romanticism; it is the expression of a last-ditch attachment to the value of the individual expressed in philosophical terms" (1987: 136–137).

Murdoch's best-known philosophical work is *The Sovereignty of Good*, 1970, consisting of three essays published earlier. Two other essential works are Murdoch's *Metaphysics as a Guide to Morals*, 1992, and the collection of her essays in *Existentialists and Mystics: Writings on Philosophy and Literature*, 1997. She published *The Fire and the Sun: Why Plato Banished the Artists* in 1977 and *Two Platonic Dialogues* in 1996.[7] Her appreciation of Plato is pervasive.

In 1968 she described herself as "a kind of Platonist."[8] In a 1978 interview, she said, "Plato is not only the father of our philosophy, he is our best philosopher" (1997: 6). In the spirit of Plato, Murdoch defended the importance of consciousness; she recognized the positive, magnetic role of goodness, rejecting the idea that goodness is just a subjective expression of individual will and desire. She asserted that the ethical reflection of her day should be replaced with a concern for love and the transforming power of beauty and good art. In her view, Plato "was concerned throughout with how people can change their lives so as to become good. The best, though not the only method for this change, is *dialectic*, that is, philosophy regarded as a spiritual discipline" (1997: 404).

Her novels won the Booker Prize, the James Tait Black Memorial Prize, and the Whitbread Literary Award, among others. Her novels have been translated into at least twenty-six languages. She was awarded honorary degrees from Cambridge University, the University of Bath, Durham

---

[7] These two works are reprinted in *Existentialists and Mystics*.
[8] Rose, "Iris Murdoch," 59–73.

University, Kingston University, and others. Queen Elizabeth II named her a Dame Commander of the Order of the British Empire in 1987 for her services to literature, hence earning the title Dame Iris Murdoch.

In 1956 Murdoch married John Bayley, an Oxford professor, writer, and literary critic. They had no children. Their marriage, many of Murdoch's relationships, and details of her life and thought are artfully portrayed in Peter J. Conradi's excellent biography *Iris Murdoch: A Life*.

In 1997 Murdoch was diagnosed with Alzheimer's disease. In 1999 she died in Oxford. Bayley wrote *Iris: A Memoir* in 1998 and *Iris and Her Friends* in 1999, offering an intimate portrayal of caring for Murdoch near the end of her life. A film called *Iris* was made in 2001.

In tribute to Murdoch's love of painting, the background of her portrait in the National Portrait Gallery, London, features a sixteenth-century painting by Titian. Murdock deemed *The Flaying of Marsyas* to be one of the greatest paintings on the human condition.

1.2 Murdoch Contra Mundum

The two oldest universities in Britain are Oxford University, founded in 1096, and Cambridge University, in 1209. In the nineteenth and twentieth centuries, other British universities (at St. Andrews, Glasgow, Edinburgh, and London, among others) were centers of important philosophical activity, but immediately following World War II, Oxford and Cambridge had some preeminence. The philosophical climate was not entirely homogenous, but there was a tangible opposition in Oxford and Cambridge to an earlier philosophical movement known as British idealism.

British idealism, a movement from the 1870s to the early 1930s, gave primacy to mind or the mental in its understanding of ultimate reality. One of its founders, Thomas Hill Green, argued that we are part of an absolute mind suffused with goodness, truth, and beauty. Francis Herbert Bradley upheld the ultimate reality of what he called "The Absolute." He said, "The Absolute is actually good, and throughout the world of goodness it is truly realized in different degrees of satisfaction. Since in ultimate Reality all existence and all thought and feeling, becomes one, we may say that every feature in the universe is thus absolutely good."[9] The grim reality of World War I and the rising tide of modern science, especially Darwinian evolution, undermined the appeal of British idealism.

---

[9] Bradley, *Appearance and Reality*, 365.

Famously, in 1903 G. E. Moore advanced an influential paper called "The Refutation of Idealism," in which he compared idealist claims with common sense. For instance, he contrasted J. M. E. McTaggart's view that time is unreal with the fact that he (Moore) had eaten breakfast earlier in the day. While Murdoch was not a British idealist, she thought some of its critics had mistakenly thrown out mind, goodness, and the British idealist critique of the individualism and laissez-faire capitalism of their day. She quipped that we need both speculative metaphysics and common sense: "McTaggart says that time is unreal. Moore replies that he has just had his breakfast. Both these aspects of philosophy are necessary to it." (1970: 1)

Another unifying factor in the intellectual climate in Murdoch's environs was a deep antipathy to Cartesian mind-body dualism. The classic work that critiqued Cartesian dualism was Gilbert Ryle's *The Concept of Mind*. Ryle described his treatment of dualism as deliberately abusive.[10] It will be useful to present Ryle's portrait of his philosophical target:

> With the doubtful exceptions of idiots and infants in arms, every human being has both a body and a mind.... Human bodies are in space and are subject to the mechanical laws which govern all other bodies in space. Bodily processes and states can be inspected by external observers. So a man's bodily life is as much of a public affair as are the lives of animals and reptiles and even as the careers of trees, crystals and planets.
>
> But minds are not in space, nor are their operations subject to mechanical laws. The workings of one mind are not witnessable by other observers, its career is private. Only I can take direct cognizance of the states and processes of my own mind. A person therefore lives through two collateral histories, one consisting of what happens in and to his body, the other consisting of what happens in and to his mind. The first is public, the second private.[11]

In Section 2, we will challenge the fairness of this portrait of mind-body dualism. For now, we simply note Ryle's depicting the mind and body as bifurcated, occupying radically different realms. Ryle treated the concept of mind as more obscure and occult compared with the common-sense solidity of the body. Indeed, Ryle's book systematically analyzed mental activity (thinking, feeling, and intending) as either bodily behavior or dispositions to act or speak. It is likely that Ryle denied he was a behaviorist because he interpreted behaviorism as denying the existence of minds.

---

[10] Ryle, *The Concept of Mind*, 15.
[11] Ibid., 11–12.

Ryle claimed to recognize the mind, but the mind can only be known and analyzed as actual and dispositional behavior. As we shall see in Section 2, Ryle denied that the mind *exists* in the same sense that bodies exist.

Iris Murdoch saw Ryle's attack on mental subjectivity as being in alliance with work by Stuart Hampshire and Ludwig Wittgenstein. Hampshire wrote, "The observer is always a self-moving body among other bodies which he observes and intentionally manipulates."[12] Murdoch saw Hampshire as depicting the mental as a mere shadow of observable bodies and not substantially real, just as a shadow of a tree is not a substantive thing itself, but the tree's blocking of light. Murdoch described Hampshire's position: "What is 'real' is potentially open to different observers. The inner or mental world is inevitably parasitic upon the outer world, it has a 'parasitic and shadowy nature.' … The play of the mind, free of any expression in audible speech or visible action is a reality, as the play of shadows is a reality" (1997: 302).

Wittgenstein's insistence that the meaning of language must be public was used in what became known as the private language argument to cast doubt on the direct private awareness of conscious states. In meaningful discourse we can correct errant usage by observation. For example, if we claimed that we had arthritis in our brain, it could be pointed out that we are misusing our terms, for arthritis involves an agitation of joints (as in the knees), whereas there are no joints in the brain. But how can we correct the use of mental terms when their referent is not observable by other people? As an aside, we note that there is still some controversy over Wittgenstein's full understanding of the mental, given his enigmatic claims such as a sensation "is not a something but it is not a nothing either."[13]

Murdoch viewed Ryle, Hampshire, and Wittgenstein as making human consciousness "a subject which no longer exists in British philosophy" (1997: 146).

Another element that needs to be identified in this depiction of the intellectual climate of Murdoch's day is the anti-metaphysics of logical positivism and its rejection of the meaningfulness of ethics, aesthetics, and religion.

---

[12] Hampshire, *Thought and Action*, 53.
[13] Wittgenstein, *Philosophical Investigations*, 304. The passage cited continues: "The conclusion was only that a nothing would serve just as well as a something about which nothing could be said." This suggests that Wittgenstein might be indifferent as to whether sensations are real. But it is possible to read him as only objecting to the idea that sensations may be privately, introspectively identified without regard to the satisfaction of verifiable public criteria (see 296, 298, 303, 304).

Logical positivism sought to restrict meaning to matters that were purely conceptual (such as the laws of logic) or what may be verified in sensory experience. This ruled out not only British idealist claims about the Absolute but also claims that purport to be meaningful in ethics, aesthetics, and religion. A. J. Ayer, one of the principle early advocates of logical positivism, held that sensory experience may verify what is the case, but not what we ought to do ethically (pursue what is right and avoid what is wrong) or what we should respond to with wonder or aversion (beauty and ugliness) or what we should worship as our creator and redeemer (God). Despite his opposition to many of Murdoch's convictions, he was not a behaviorist or reductive materialist.

At Oxford and Cambridge, many philosophers construed ethical judgments as the expression of preferences, a function of what a person desires or wills. R. M. Hare of Oxford sought to retain some normativity (or meaning) in ethics by specifying the conditions in which we express our will and desires. For example, our ostensible will and desire may be tarnished by false information. You may think you want nuclear disarmament among all nations, but because your deepest desire is to promote world peace and (let us imagine) nuclear disarmament is not the best path to world peace, your current desire conflicts with what you deeply desire. So, many philosophers sought to refine our moral reflection, but they were mostly concerned with external decision-making and action. They were not focused on traditional virtues such as practical wisdom, friendship, and proper pride (as expounded by Aristotle and his followers). They tended to be utilitarian (one should do that act that promotes the greatest utility, usually understood as happiness or desire-satisfaction).

In Murdoch's day, there were Oxford Christian philosophers and theologians – Basil Mitchell, Austin Farrer, John Lucas, and Ian Ramsey, among others. Murdoch presented to the Oxford Socratic Club, where C. S. Lewis, a literary scholar as well as a popular Christian writer, served as president from 1942 to 1954. But the general consensus was averse to Christianity and religion. Ayer was so convinced that theism was meaningless that for most of his life he would not describe himself as an atheist, because he thought that might suggest that he believed theism was a meaningful possibility.

1.3 An Overview of Murdoch's Philosophy

Murdoch challenged the orthodoxy of her day. She argued against the sufficiency of public, quasi-behavioristic accounts of persons. The view of Ryle et al. needed to be transcended. "The 'world' of *The Concept of Mind* is the world in which people play cricket, cook cakes, make simple decisions, remember their childhood and go to the circus, not the world in which they commit sins, fall in love, say prayers or join the Communist Party" (1987: 78–79). While not a self-described dualist, Murdoch lamented the way some philosophers rejected Descartes' insistence on the evident reality of ourselves as individual subjects capable of free, morally responsible vision and action.

Throughout much of her work, Murdoch was skeptical about the widespread distinction between facts and values, or the distinction between *what is the case* and *what ought to be the case*. In her view, the world we experience is suffused with values. Ethics and aesthetics are not mere projections of what we will or desire. By lovingly attending to other persons and to the beauty around us, we can be transformed so that our will and desires can be challenged and renounced to make way for a moral rebirth. "The area of morals, and ergo of moral philosophy, can now be seen, not as a hole-and-corner matter of debts and promises, but as covering the whole of our mode of living and the quality of our relations with the world" (1970: 95).

Murdoch, along with her female philosopher friends Anscombe, Foot, and Midgley, opposed the utilitarianism of their day and promoted ethical reflection that included attention to virtues, moral development, and love. A long-term theme for Murdoch is a critique of egoism. She developed a case for the importance of setting aside narrow egotistical concerns and the importance of (using a term inspired by Simone Weil) "unselfing." This involves persons transcending their narrow self-concerns.

Our book is titled *Iris Murdoch and the Transcendent* because she believed we need to transcend the restricted parameters of her day through thinking about minds and what is valuable. She believed we need to transcend self-interest. We need to be open to transcending our judgments of one another, prepared to revise or alter our misjudgments of one another. We use the term "transcend" here to refer to what Murdoch believes we must surpass or move beyond.[14]

There is a broader sense of transcendence we wish to explore. As we have noted, Murdoch rejected traditional theism. The following passage from *The Sovereignty of Good* seems to leave no room for some transcendent,

---

[14] Bridget Clarke refers to Murdoch's view that other persons "transcend – are not fully captured by – one's grasp of them at any given moment" as "the ordinary transcendent" as distinct from supernatural transcendence (Clarke, 2018: 253). George Steiner uses the term "immanent transcendence" to describe Murdoch's "down to earth rapture or illumination" (Steiner, 1999: xiv).

divine reality or an impersonal, purposive reality that may account for why the cosmos exists (or, in Murdoch's terminology, why we are here).

> There are properly many patterns and purposes in life, but there is no general and as it were externally guaranteed pattern or purpose of the kind for which philosophers and theologians used to search. We are what we seem to be, transient mortal creatures subject to necessity and chance. That is to say, there is, in my view, no God in the traditional sense of that term…. Equally the various metaphysical substitutes for God – Reason, Science, History – are false deities. Our destiny can be examined but it cannot be justified or totally explained. We are simply here. And if there is any kind of sense or unity in human life, and the dream of this does not cease to haunt us, it is of some other kind and must be sought within a human experience which has nothing outside it. (1970: 77)

Murdoch did not share the disdain for religion that many of her contemporaries like Sartre and Ayer had. Unlike Sartre, she did not have what she called his religious hatred for religion. It would be shocking to find in any of Sartre's or Ayer's work an appeal to the Bible in support of their views; not so with Murdoch citing Philippians 4:8: "Whatsoever things are true, whatsoever things are honest, whatsoever things are just, whatsoever things are pure, whatsoever things are lovely, whatsoever things of good report, if there be any virtue and if there be any praise – meditate on these things" (1970: 55). Unlike Ayer, she engaged the work of many Christian figures such as St. Paul, Augustine, Anselm, Eckhart, Julian of Norwich, Kierkegaard, and Gabriel Marcel. She took the ontological argument for the existence of God seriously. She was at home addressing many religious themes: understanding that life can be a pilgrimage and that there is value in religious practices such as self-examination, confession, forgiveness, prayer, and meditation. Her concept of God as a great work of art could not be further from Ayer's (1993: 31). She treated Hinduism, Buddhism, and Taoism with philosophical respect.

We find it surprising that Murdoch stated so emphatically in *The Sovereignty of Good* that the purpose and patterns that philosophers and theologians "used to search" for are no longer valid. Murdoch wrote that finding sense about human life "must be sought within a human experience which has nothing outside it." In the last section of this Element, we will ask what Murdoch might mean about what is within or external to human experience and whether she offers compelling reasons behind where we must or must not look for "any kind of sense or unity in human life." We will also ask if her values would be strengthened if rooted in some form of Platonic theism or a nontheistic purposive reality.

2 The Importance of Being Conscious

> We need a moral philosophy in which the concept of love, so rarely mentioned now by philosophers, can once again be made central.
>
> Iris Murdoch (1970: 45)

The reality of consciousness is the salient factor grounding all the work of Iris Murdoch. None of her insights about goodness, love, art, imagination, and personal transformation make sense if we are not conscious, thinking, feeling beings capable of self-reflection and responsive to other persons and the world. Murdoch was not a traditional mind-body dualist, but she shared with dualists a dissatisfaction with the quasi-behaviorism and the dismissal or marginalization of subjective inner life that she found in work by Ryle, Hampshire, and Wittgenstein. Although she wrote "my own temperament inclines to monism," evidently in contrast to dualism, she did not think of our inner life as homogeneous or the very same thing as observable brain states (1970: 49). Her major contribution on this point has been too frequently ignored in the history of philosophy.

In this section, let us first analyze the hostility to mind-dualism. We do so because the same criticism that dualism faced would apply to Murdoch's defense of the reality of conscious, subjective states not reducible to physical states and behavior. We then present and defend Murdoch's case for the reality of conscious experience. As this section focuses on Murdoch's critique of Ryle's overreaction against Descartes' view of the self, we conclude with reflections on Murdoch's view that Derridean structuralism also overreacts against Descartes and Cartesianism. By her lights, Derrida's rejection of Descartes leads him to submerge the individual into a sea of language. Using very different philosophical tools, Ryle and Derrida deny what Murdoch takes to be basic about our subjective, conscious individual lives.

2.1 Who Is Afraid of Mind-Body Dualism?

Her contemporaries feared that mind-body dualism saddled us with an absurd bifurcation of persons into two entities, at odds with common sense and ordinary language. Many critics also thought that the definition of mind-body dualism developed by Descartes in the seventeenth century fostered a damaging, perhaps irrefutable skepticism about the external world and other minds. Once you insist on the certain, perhaps indubitable reality of private subjective experience, why trust that the external, public world is as it appears? More specifically, why trust that what appears to be other people are actually other people and not just zombies or automatons or illusions? The Wittgensteinian philosopher David Pears proposed that dualism can lead one to believe that our subjective life is like a prison from which there is no reasonable, philosophical escape.[15] Wittgenstein himself suggested that the Cartesian position amounts to a situation in which individuals have their own individual boxes with beetles in each of them that only the individual can observe (Wittgenstein, 1953: 293). The absurdity of such a metaphorical picture, with its slightly grotesque features (assuming one does not relish the idea that each person harbors a kind of invisible insect), contributed to thinking that mind-body dualism was contrary to common sense and ordinary language, absurd or comic, and perhaps grotesque.[16]

In assessing the philosophical landscape, it first needs to be appreciated how Ryle and others came to attack a caricature of dualism, a straw man.

Let us return to Ryle's depiction of mind-body dualism cited in Section 1. Ryle suggested that dualists might make exceptions for nonhuman animals and infants in arms. Descartes did deny that nonhuman animals had minds or souls, but most dualists from Plato to contemporary dualists do not.[17] And virtually none affirm that infants are mindless. Ryle proposed that dualists affirm that we live two lives, harnessed together. "Harnessed" is an odd term, suggesting enchainment of some kind between two physical entities, whereas most dualists treat mind-body interaction as a basic, evident causal relationship. Most dualists treat embodied persons as functioning as whole beings. Healthy persons act as whole beings in the spatial, public world – speaking, acting, sleeping, and waking in a world where they work, play, procreate, write novels, suffer, and so on. If dualism is true in a healthy embodiment, there is no gulf between the mental and physical. But a gulf can appear in cases of ethical or physical–mental fracture.

When we are deceptive and harbor unexpressed hostility, there can be a gap between what you observe of us in our public life and what we are really thinking and feeling. And in cases of severe brain damage, we may lose control over our bodies, in which case they can appear to be our container or prison. So, when anti-dualists propose that dualists leave us with our bodies being akin to machines inhabited by ghosts (minds or souls),

---

[15] Pears, *The False Prison.*

[16] It has been observed that the beetle in the box analogy is less than perfect, given Wittgenstein's anti-Cartesianism, as the analogy posits actual things (beetles) that are incommunicable or ineffable. But part of Wittgenstein's case against Cartesianism is that it posits things that cannot be identified by public, verifiable criteria.

[17] Loose et al. (eds.), *The Blackwell Companion to Substance Dualism.*

they overlook cases when this can be an accurate description of how mind-body integration can go wrong. Sadly, even Wittgenstein's beetle thought experiment can occur, as in the cases described by neurologist Oliver Sacks in his 1973 book *Awakenings*. Sacks described victims of the encephalitis lethargica epidemic as having mental states they are unable to share or express until being treated with an experimental drug. Absent the drug (which was only partially successful), persons might be in Wittgenstein's predicament, though (according to Sacks) the patients had feelings and thoughts that were not observable.[18]

The idea that mind-body dualism ushers in an unacceptable skepticism would not vex Murdoch. Under ordinary conditions (apart from philosophy of mind), she was doubtful about our certain, precise knowledge of one another.

> Mr. Hare says briskly that individuals (and doubtless situations) 'can be described as fully and precisely as we wish'. Now, with the best will in the world, this is not always so. There are situations that are obscure and people who are incomprehensible, and the moral agent, as well as the artist, may find himself unable to describe something which in some sense he apprehends. (1997: 90)

If Murdoch is right, we should not rule out the possibility of skepticism concerning other minds. While we may set aside thought experiments that other people are zombies as science fiction, we do well to question whether our grasp of the mental states of others (as well as our own mental states) is infallible and incorrigible.

Histories of philosophy that chronicle the challenge to dualism usually include important milestones like Thomas Nagel's famous 1974 essay "What is it like to be a bat?" In that essay, Nagel contends that a complete knowledge of a bat's anatomy and behavior would not inform us of the experience of what it is like to be a bat. While Nagel did not argue for dualism, he sought to discourage the dismissal of experience in favor of materialistic reductionism. T. L. S. Sprigge likewise proposed that an exhaustive account of a person's brain would not reveal anything about that person's thoughts and experience. The philosophy of mind literature would go on to develop anti-reductive arguments involving modal thought experiments (including zombies, out-of-body experiences, and arguments about how

---

[18] Sacks' patients might be likened to Galen Strawson's "weather watchers" – imaginary beings with mental states but no capacity for any behavior or language to express their mental states (Strawson, 1994). Strawson used this thought experiment in his case against neobehaviorist accounts of the mental, including what he took to be a common interpretation of Wittgenstein's position.

2.2 Fearless Consciousness

In April 1964, Murdoch published "The Idea of Perfection," based on a lecture she gave in 1962. In this paper, later republished in the collection *The Sovereignty of Good*, Murdoch took issue with her contemporaries who treat the mental as a mere shadow world, something we can discard unless the mental is expressed or analyzed in terms of language and action. Her main target in that essay was Stuart Hampshire, especially in his book *Thought and Action*, but it could just as well be have been Ryle or Wittgenstein. In her essay, Murdoch developed a thought experiment in which a woman's behavior, speech, and all manifest material aspects of her being remain constant. And yet, Murdoch contended that we can readily imagine that the woman undergoes a very real and ethically significant change. She transitions from being hostile to her daughter-in-law to being empathetic and accepting, even loving.

We cite Murdoch's thought experiment at length:

> A mother, whom I shall call M, feels hostility to her daughter-in-law, whom I shall call D. M finds D quite a good-hearted girl, but while not exactly common yet certainly unpolished and lacking in dignity and refinement. D is inclined to be pert and familiar, insufficiently ceremonious, brusque, sometimes positively rude, always tiresomely juvenile. M does not like D's accent or the way D dresses. M feels that her son has married beneath him. Let us assume for the purposes of the example that the mother, who is a very 'correct' person, behaves beautifully to the girl throughout, not allowing her real opinion to appear in any way. We might underline this aspect of the example by supposing that the young couple have emigrated or that D is now dead: the point being to ensure that whatever is in question as *happening* happens entirely in M's mind.
>
> This much for M's first thoughts about D. Time passes, and it could be that M settles down with a hardened sense of grievance and a fixed picture of D, imprisoned (if I may use a question-begging word) by the cliché: my poor son has married a silly vulgar girl. However, the M of the example is an intelligent and well-intentioned person, capable of self-criticism, capable of giving careful and just *attention* to an object which confronts her. M tells herself: 'I am old-fashioned and conventional. I may be prejudiced and narrow-minded. I may be snobbish. I am certainly jealous. Let me look again.' Here I assume M observes D or at least reflects deliberately about D, until gradually, her vision of

> D alters. If we take D to be now absent or dead this can make it clear that the change is not in D's behavior but in M's mind. D is discovered to be not vulgar but refreshingly simple, not undignified but spontaneous, not noisy but gay, not tiresomely juvenile but delightfully youthful, and so on. And as I say, *ex hypothesi*, M's outward behavior, beautiful from the start, in no way alters. (1970: 16–17)

In her essay, Murdoch did not make the claim that she was original in pointing out how there can be very real, non-shadowy processes that go on mentally that are not captured by a behaviorist point of view. But she was the first, or among the first, to deploy her thesis in the way of a thought experiment in postwar English philosophical literature. Of course, she takes herself to be articulating what is widely known to each of us in our interior struggles, but she is among the first to charge that such common subjective experiences were not taken seriously by Ryle and his colleagues.

Murdoch pointed out that the supposedly spurious inner life (targeted by Ryle) has been widely recognized in spiritual practices of repentance, as when persons may profess to repent of their sin, but still not be certain that they have truly repented. She opted not to use a religious example to make her point, lest this raises special concerns in the philosophy of religion, but she does not shy away from referring to love as a real, elementary goal in life, religious or secular. The mother-in-law M is seeking or comes to succeed in loving the daughter-in-law D. In sum, Murdoch's case for a nonbehavioristic account of the mental comes down to a case for recognizing the reality and importance of love. So, prior to Nagel and company, Murdoch developed a narrative of a person's values and perspective shifting through an inner dialogue, affirming the reality of evident, emotional states that resist analysis in terms of public, overt behavior and language. None of the other well-documented objections to the behaviorist movement against the mental make an overt case on the grounds of the reality and importance of love.

Murdoch's "The Idea of Perfection" essay has been appreciated for drawing attention to the ethical importance of our interior states, thus challenging the mid-twentieth-century moral philosophy focus on action and rules that should guide decision-making. But just as important is her affirmation that we persons have inner states and lives not covered by public behavioral analyses. It needs restating that she did not claim that persons have infallible access to their mental states. One may be genuinely perplexed about whether one is loving a person or has truly repented a sin. Our lack of infallible access to the mental should no more diminish recognizing the reality of the mental than our lack of infallible access to the world around us should lead us to worry whether we are victims of a massive hallucination.

To be clear, Murdoch was not a self-described mind-body or Cartesian dualist. But she is affirming the reality of consciousness that was under fire:

> If I suddenly make a decision, or solve a problem, though I were to die the next moment it would still be true that a particular mental movement was made. Such mental events are *there*, God sees them, and they are just as compact and determinate as physical events, though possibly harder to describe. (1997: 46)

2.3 Welcome to Your Inner Life

Appreciating Murdoch's essay invites us to a very different point of view than those of Hampshire, Ryle, and her other contemporaries. Appreciating how very different it is becomes even more vivid when comparing Murdoch's position to Ryle's famous case of seeking to discount any appeal to the mental beyond overt behavior.

Ryle contended that when you consider the sentence "she came into the room in a flood of tears," this should not be considered as real and straightforward as the claim "she came into the room in a box."[19] Ryle claims that both sentences may be true, but then he goes on to claim that their truth is not a univocal or straightforward matter:

> It is perfectly proper to say, in one logical tone of voice, that there exist minds, and to say, in another tone of voice that there exists bodies. But these expressions do not indicate two different species of existence, for 'existence' is not a generic word like 'colored' or 'sexed.' They indicate two different senses of 'exist', somewhat as 'rising' has different senses in 'the tide is rising', 'hopes are rising' and 'the average age of death is rising.' A man would be thought to be making a poor joke who said that three things were now rising, namely the tide, hopes and the average age of death. It would be just as good or bad a joke to say that there exist prime numbers and Wednesdays and public opinions and navies; or that there exist both minds and bodies.[20]

There are two problems here.

The first is that Ryle seems to conflate claims about what exists and claims about what makes the claims true. In his first example about "rising," each claim is, in principle, worthy of being considered true (what exists), but

---

[19] Ryle, *The Concept of Mind*, 22.
[20] Ryle, *The Concept of Mind*, 23.

obviously in recognizing their truth, one is not committed to positing that there is an observable thing, such as "the average age." An average age, like the average plumber, is a mathematical calculation about a median number. As H. D. Lewis pointed out in reply to Ryle, his effort to assimilate mental states to abstractions like "the average age" creates a confusion of categories about what constitutes the mental. The evident reality of the mental is no less real (or existing) than bodily processes. "Mental processes are real, they 'are' or they go on just as physical ones do."[21]

In Ryle's second set of examples, we suggest that they should not motivate us to think that each of the items involves a different sort of existence. We propose one should claim that there are prime numbers, Wednesdays, public opinions, and navies, with no equivocation about the status of "being" or claiming what exists, but then offer one's best account of prime numbers (we happen to adopt a Platonic account of numbers, but one might offer a nominalist account), calendar times, public opinion is presumably some generalization about the opinion of people in a community, and navies involve a particular military incorporation as distinct from, say, armies and church groups.

Ryle gives us no reason to think we are equivocating when we claim that "bodies exist" and "there are persons with internal emotions that lead them to cry." If there is a joke in play in Ryle's claim here, it is to infer that minds and bodies are not equally real, based on a person stringing together such odd examples of what there is. A little imagination might help make the examples Ryle uses less strange. Consider this statement that seems (to us) meaningful: As the tide was rising, Jones started hoping he would be rescued and not drown like the average person in his position. Or: On the 7th of April, a Wednesday, public opinion wavered about whether the government should increase its funding for the navy.

A second problem with Ryle's perspective is revealed in his discounting the existence or truth-value of a woman coming into a room "in a flood of tears." Why think a woman "in distress" should be less real than a body "in a box"? Of course, the term "flood" in the sentence is a metaphor, not literal. But most English speakers would readily interpret this as a claim about the intensity of the weeping. Does Ryle think the existence of a weeping woman is not as straightforward and ontologically secure as the movement of boxes? Apart from the obvious distinction between when "in" refers to a state or process (weeping, perhaps grieving) and when it refers to a physical enclosure, the cases seem on the same footing as far as

---

[21] Lewis, *The Elusive Mind*, 43.

making truth-claims. Discounting a woman's stress seems at least modestly insensitive to what is truly at issue and what should be the focus of loving attention. Ryle's thesis seems derogatory.

As for the danger of skepticism, we noted earlier that Murdoch would not have worried that recognizing the reality of our inner lives may lead to radical skepticism. Recall that she did not assume we have infallible, incorrigible knowledge of our inner lives and only a sketchy grasp of the people around us and the world. She did not just allow for self-deception; she described it in her novels (for example, the self-deluded Charles Arrowby in *The Sea, The Sea*). Murdoch thought that a kind of Cartesian solipsism was possible due to ethical reasons, as when Sartre contended that love between persons is chimerical and pronounced that hell is other people (1987: 14). Murdoch thought that our natural self-centeredness makes it difficult for a person to realize that other people are truly real (1997: 228). In her view, someone who professes to be ignorant of the feelings of others is more likely to be suffering from egotism rather than from adopting a dodgy philosophy of mind.[22]

A promising way to locate Murdoch's philosophy of mind is to see her as affirming the reality of consciousness and our capacity to move from spite to love as essential facts about us. She sides with Sartre against Ryle when it comes to salvaging consciousness:

> Sartre remains interested in the deliverances of consciousness because of the role which our conceptualizings of ourselves play in relation to our conduct; and the feature of our awareness which for Ryle marks the inner world beyond salvage is for Sartre its most important feature. (1987: 115)

But Murdoch rejected Sartre's analysis of consciousness because he did not consider the love of goodness and beauty. The importance of Murdoch's defense for her other convictions cannot be overestimated:

> We need the concept of consciousness to understand how morality is cognitive, how there is no ubiquitous gulf fixed between fact and value, intellect and will. Reflection on this concept enables us to display how deeply, subtly and in detail, values, the various qualities and grades between good and bad, 'seep' through our moment-to-moment experiences ... value, valuing, is not a specialized activity of the will, but an apprehension of the world, an aspect of cognition, which is everywhere. (1993: 265)

---

[22] Murdoch may have influenced Stanley Cavell, who also turned the problem of other minds into a moral rather than theoretical matter (Cavell, 2015).

We should add that Murdoch's philosophy of the self and our capacity to make morally responsible choices was, in her view, a basic datum, evident in our experience of ourselves. Worldviews that promote determinism (in some versions of Marxism, Freudianism, and the natural sciences) all miss something: "our dense, familiar inner stuff, private and personal, with a quality and a value of its own, something which we can scrutinise and control" (1993: 153). She suggested that the lure of freedom-denying determinism lies in our desire to escape the ordinary, evident fact of our moral accountability for who we are and how we live. We can scrutinize and control how we see other people, just as M changed her view of D. Murdoch wrote:

> We are not, in ordinary life as opposed to philosophy, determinists; and in philosophy a doctrine of total determinism has never been intelligibly stated. What we have to deal with in philosophy is a ghost of determinism, which finds support in various nonphilosophical desires to believe that 'it cannot be otherwise'. (1993: 153)

Murdoch diagnosed the effort by Marxists and Freudians to dismiss human freedom as part of their effort to deny the reality and significance of ourselves as individuals. Marx famously depicted persons as ensembles of social relations. Murdoch wrote:

> But surely the 'person' we wish to defend here, endorsed by commonsense, is not so easily magicked away. Our present moment, our experiences, our flow of consciousness, our indelible moral sense, are not all these essentially linked together and do they not *imply* the individual? (1993: 153)

From a Murdochian perspective, it is by studying the transition from spite and disdain of one individual (M) of another (D) to a transformative love appreciation (M's coming to cherish D) that we realize the inescapable importance of our inner lives.

It is worth noting that in the twentieth century, the philosophy of mind had only gradually seen love's relevance to the theory of values. True, theories of personal identity have been used to advance or attack utilitarianism and ethical egoism, in debates over animal consciousness and in some medical ethics, but a great deal of energy has focused on metaphysics (is thinking a brain process?) and epistemology (can we trust what appears to be the first-person point of view versus the third-person view of science?). If philosophers of mind had followed Murdoch's methodology, perhaps history would have altered and included more attention on how the philosophy of mind overlaps with the philosophy of love.

In Murdoch's philosophy, individuals live in a world that is suffused with values they did not create. Under the influence of existentialism or Humean naturalism, we may believe that we are the creators of values, but this conflicts with the reality of ordinary experience prior to being corrupted by unwarranted philosophical assumptions. Being determined by our social circumstances, we have a tendency to long for consoling fantasies, which can overcome us; it takes courage to rise above such forces and to focus our loving attention on what is good. Murdoch thought courageous resistance should also be shown in light of structuralism and deconstructionism.

2.4 Another Warning About the Loss of the Conscious Individual

Murdoch believed we should resist having our conscious individuality marginalized, not just in the context of behaviorism, Marxism et al., but also in the context of work by structuralists and deconstructionists regarding concepts of "self." According to Murdoch, structuralists and deconstructionists deflated questions about metaphysical transcendence. Jacques Derrida and associates were described by Murdoch as driven by hostility to Plato and the metaphysical tradition in the West, especially the work of Descartes. The structuralists focused on language, rather than a reality independent of language. Murdoch wrote:

> As [their] doctrine it might be called Linguistic Idealism, Linguistic Monism, or Linguistic Determinism, since it presents a picture of the individual as submerged in language, rather than as an autonomous user of language. (1993: 185)

She proposes that the turn to linguistics was motivated, in part, by a widespread rejection of Descartes' concept of the self as a subject who thinks (feels, acts, and senses). Descartes famously advanced the *cogito* (Latin for "I think") and the *cogito, ergo sum* ("I think, therefore I am"). What Murdoch said of atheism, she might have said of the rejection of the self as a real individual: It is one thing to say there is no individual self; it is another thing to believe it and its consequences. She said:

> He, Derrida, following 'logical' implications of the rejection of *cogito*, concludes that if there can be no solitary knower ... then there can, really, be no knower, only a network of meanings (the infinitely great net of language itself) under which there is nothing.... Because of the vast extent of language and the way in which meanings of words and concepts are determined by innumerable relationships with other words and concepts, no individual speaker can really 'know' what he means, we are *unconscious* of the immediate linguistic beyond which we think

that we 'use' when really it is using us. That is, in rejecting Descartes' *argument,* Derrida *also* rejects the *concept* of the autonomous individual; and with it the (ordinary) concept of truth. (1993: 187)

According to Murdoch, the price of Derrida's account is too high: It involves a rejection of the idea that we are individuals who use language who are free to lovingly pursue the true, the Good, and the beautiful. "Value, morality is removed by the structuralist picture if taken seriously" (1993: 190). Far from being truly emancipatory, "structuralism is in effect a new-fashioned determinism" (1993: 203).

Murdoch's views on structuralism and deconstruction demonstrate that – contrary to some of her critics, who worried the Platonic good might draw her too far away from mortal humans and their flaws – she did recognize the importance of real-life individuals.[23] Murdoch's views would have no force in the absence of valuing real-life individuals.

We now turn to Murdoch's theory of values, which stands out in sharp contrast to her intellectual milieu.

3 The Transcendent, Transformative Power of Goodness

> The freedom which is the proper human goal is the freedom from fantasy, that is the realism of compassion. What I have called fantasy, the proliferation of blinding self-centered aims and images, is itself a powerful system of energy, and most of what is often called 'will' or 'willing' belongs to this system. What counteracts the system is attention to reality inspired by, consisting of, love.
>
> Iris Murdoch (1970: 65)

The term "love" in English today is used very broadly; for a person may be said to love the well-being and flourishing of another person or to love dominating others and using them for their own egotistic satisfaction. The kind of love that Murdoch is passionate to articulate and promote is a love that is in response to the goodness of others, the world, and oneself (proper self-love, rather than vanity). Ultimately this involves our receptivity to changing our "naturally selfish" (1970: 76) desires and willful self-obsession.

We begin by describing the widespread fact/value distinction sketched in Section 1 and then describe Murdoch's radical challenge to such a "dubious" framework (1987: 69). We then turn to her account of life as a pilgrimage and conclude with her challenging the contemporary, binary view of gender.

---

[23] Nussbaum, "Love and Vision: Iris Murdoch on Eros and the Individual," 29–53.

3.1 A World of Facts and Invented Values

The fact/value distinction has lived many philosophical lives. One can find the distinction in David Hume's 1739 *Treatise of Human Nature*. In G. E. Moore's 1903 *Principia Ethica*, inferring values from facts is called the "naturalistic fallacy." Moore thought that no statements about facts (even the fact that someone is happy) entail that such facts or events are good. Moore thought that any fact still invites the question: But is it good? As far back as Plato, we find a suggestion that goodness eludes many ostensible facts. For example, in the dialogue the Euthyphro, we are asked whether even the command of God or a god is good.

We suggest that the rise of modern science played a part in promoting the distinction between facts and values. Arguably, Galileo and Newton were describing and explaining a material world without the use of value-laden terms like "good" and "bad," "right" and "wrong," and "beauty" and "ugliness." They may have thought that the creation was good and beautiful, but such thoughts were not part of their scientific method. The concept of love may enter into an account of the motion of two humans (Romeo and Juliet), but it has no place in Newton's laws of motion.

Murdoch saw the distinction between fact and value as pervasive in modern thought, including Wittgenstein's influential first book, *Tractatus Logico-Philosophicus* (1993: 31). A host of postwar philosophers contended that evaluative terms such as "good" and "bad" and "evil" should be analyzed in terms of the preferences (the will or desire) of persons. For you to profess finding something wrong (killing innocent persons, slavery) is for you to express your disapproval or revulsion about such acts. Philosophers like R. M. Hare thought that such a preference theory of ethics could still account for why many believe that ethics can be a subject of meaningful debate. We can challenge each other about whether our preferences are based on false beliefs or whether our preferences are coherent or consistent. Some of our preferences could lead us to endorse intolerable consequences.

Murdoch found the fact/value distinction and Hare's attempt to preserve some meaningfulness in moral discourse to be woefully inadequate.

3.2 The Ubiquity and Power of Goodness

Murdoch thought that the fact/value distinction was in radical conflict with our moral experience. While we are by nature often self-serving and egocentric, when we are confronted by goodness, we are confronted with something with magnetic power, something that draws us out of our infantile self-preoccupation. She claimed that her colleagues who were skeptical about the authority of goodness were in radical conflict with experience. In *The Sovereignty of Good*, she wrote:

> [I] suggest that at the level of serious common sense and of an ordinary non-philosophical reflection about the nature of morals it is perfectly obvious that goodness is connected with knowledge: not with impersonal quasi-scientific knowledge of the ordinary world, whatever that may be, but with a refined and honest perception of what is really the case, a patient and just discernment and exploration of what confronts one, which is the result not simply of opening one's eyes but of a certainly perfectly familiar kind of mental discipline. (1970: 37)

Her distinction between just opening one's eyes versus reflective awareness can be illustrated crudely: You may only have to open your eyes to identify that you are seeing something red, but earnest loving attention to seeing that a soldier stabbing a baby and making it bleed to death (such as the act of infanticide by a soldier described in Dostoevsky's *Brothers Karamazov*, Part I, Book V, chapter 4) should lead a person to see such an act as wicked, the wrongful violation of a person of inexhaustible value. As this is a case that is shockingly extreme, we add a more subtle, yet powerful recognition of goodness in a different novel by Dostoevsky, *Crime and Punishment*. A student, Rodion Raskolnikov, dreams of committing the perfect crime. He kills two women with an ax. This seems as outrageously wrong as the infanticide, but what is more subtle is the way Sonia, a dispossessed person, shows such great love for Raskolnikov that he is led to confess his crime. Her love and faith enable his regeneration. She cares so much for him she accompanies him to Siberia, where he is to serve an eight-year sentence. She displays what Murdoch referred to as the "magnetic pull" of goodness that challenges us to renounce our contemptuous disregard of others (1970: 41). In Sonia's kindness to Raskolnikov and other prisoners, she comes to be known as Little Mother Sonia.

Murdoch proposed that our temptation to think that facts do not include values stems from a mistaken assumption that the facts discovered by the natural sciences make up the whole world of facts. This assumption is false, for the world described in the natural sciences is impersonal and does not include what is a crucial fact: There are persons who apprehend and respond to real values (1970: 25). Philosophers who think values contaminate the pure world of facts have fallen prey to a dangerous, ultimately false domination of science (1970: 26). It is false because the natural sciences themselves are unintelligible without scientists who are driven by values. Scientists value evidence, truth, reason, reliable observation, collaboration, and trust in their pursuit of valued goals, from curing cancer to space exploration. A comprehensive list of facts of what exists should not exclude facts about how such a list might be made, understood, or valued. In other words, *values are facts*. Some of us may have mistaken values, just as some of us may be mistaken about the facts revealed by the natural sciences. The possibility of having made a mistake about values suggests there is also a possibility of not being mistaken.

Murdoch's moral realism appealed to ordinary experience and moral psychology. Her view was like that of many twentieth-century moral realists in the phenomenological tradition, such as Max Scheler and Dietrich von Hildebrand. But Murdoch's moral realism was perhaps more relational than some of these phenomenologists. "My work is a progressive revelation of something which exists independent of me" (1970: 87). She said:

> We all, not only can but *have to* experience and deal with a transcendent reality, the resistant otherness of other persons, other things, history, the natural world, the cosmos, and this involves perpetual effort. We are amazing creatures; no wonder Sophocles calls us *deinos* [Greek for *terrible, dreadful*]. Most of this effort is moral effort. This is the sense in which morality (value) is transcendental, concerned with the conditions of experience. (1993: 268)

She affirmed the reality of the Good or goodness, not as an inference as we find in arguments for God's existence, but as revealed experientially:

> If someone says 'Do you believe that the Idea of the Good exists?' I reply, 'No, not as people used to think that God existed.' All one can do is to appeal to certain areas of experience pointing out certain features, and using suitable metaphors and inventing suitable concepts where necessary to make these features visible. (1970: 73)

Two further points are worth adding for emphasis.

First, Murdoch suggested that the alternative view that we create values through our choices and desires is contrary to common sense. "The ordinary person does not, unless corrupted by philosophy, believe that he creates values by his choices" (1970: 95). To offer a personal example, we are writing this Element because we find Murdoch's work valuable, rather than we think Murdoch's work is valuable due to our creative invention or desire. Are games a good counter-example? Games are inventions in which some things come to have value that would otherwise be baffling. Why would hitting a ball with a stick in order for the ball to fall into a hole be valuable unless it was part of a rule-governed activity called golf?

We can make the distribution of colored cards valuable if we participate in card games. But games themselves contribute to evident values such as developing athletic skills; making playful uses of memory, drama, and reason; cultivating community, and so on. Creating values *ex nihilo* or arbitrarily seems implausible. It appears that we discover, rather than invent, for example, the good of nutrition, breathing, and mobility. We go on to see the value of learning, communication, familial relations, science, sex, reproduction, and so on. This is not to diminish the role of inventions and institutions in shaping our practices of eating, breathing, mobility, communicating, or in shaping our idea of family, science, sexuality, reproduction, and the like. But moral realists like Murdoch see this as shaping something we already experience as intrinsically valuable or worthwhile, as opposed to values being created capriciously.

An important qualification needs to be added: As a moral realist, Murdoch endorsed the view that we can be mistaken in what we claim to be intrinsically valuable. For a non-realist in ethics, there is no such appeal to right and wrong. At least in a crude form of non-realism, the person who says "physician-assisted suicide is wrong" is saying "I condemn physician-assisted suicide," which is different from, but not in contradiction to, someone else who says "physician-assisted suicide is sometimes good," meaning "I do not condemn all cases of physician-assisted suicides." For the non-realist, the two people may both be right or wrong depending on the circumstances – one disapproves of physician-assisted suicide and the other approves of some physician-assisted suicides. For moral realists like Murdoch, there are truths about what one should and should not approve, even if, *or especially if*, we can have mistaken views on what is right and wrong.

A second, related point is that Murdoch suggested that the burden of proof (the *onus probandi*) lies with those who deny moral realism:

> But, why can morality not be thought of as attached to the substance of the world? Surely many people who are not philosophers, and who cannot be accused of using faulty arguments since they use no arguments, do think of their morality in just this way? They think of it as continuous with some sort of larger structure of reality, whether this be a religious structure, or a social or historical one. (1997: 65)

Consider two objections.

Perhaps Murdoch's case against the fact/value distinction rested largely on grammar, rather than an appeal to experience and ordinary practice. As Murdoch pointed out, much of our language is evaluative (1997: 27).

Could it be that our values are so interwoven with factual observations that the fact/value distinction becomes blurred linguistically? Terms like "being rude" and "being cruel" are only used when speakers find some behavior appalling or revolting. Suppose the speaker observes someone talking too loud at a restaurant and therefore judges that person to be rude, or the speaker observes someone striking a companion without apparent cause and thus judges the hit to be cruel. But the behavior of the loud person and the striker could be seen and described in a value-free manner.

Murdoch might well have replied that the objector needs to provide reasons for why our value-laden language is *merely* a grammatical convention and not a reflection that values are observable facts. Arguably, a value-free description of either behavior would seem robotic or inhumane. This becomes increasingly apparent if the behavior is exaggerated: Imagine the rudeness involves shouting obscene racist, sexist language, or the person strikes the companion multiple times while laughing.

Writing off the experience of values as a linguistic matter seems akin to writing off the certainty each of us has that we exist as only a linguistic matter. Murdoch's friend Elizabeth Anscombe did something like this when she claimed that the (Cartesian) belief that the first-person "I" refers to a self is merely a "grammatical illusion."[24] As Anscombe's critics have pointed out, she failed to show that our certain self-awareness is *merely* a grammatical or linguistic matter.[25] Murdoch herself took our self-awareness to be a basic, morally important fact. We can fall prey to illusions about ourselves, but that is different from claiming that we are illusions.

The second objection may be called the Tibetan objection. In *Morals as a Guide to Metaphysics*, Murdoch tells us a Tibetan story: A mother asks her son, who is going on a journey, to return with a religious relic. He forgets her request until he is nearly home. He sees a dog's tooth by the road. He presents the dog's tooth to his mother, reporting that it is the relic of a saint. In the following passage Murdoch appears to claim that when the inauthentic relic is placed in a chapel and made the object of loving devotion, it can gain value. This appears contrary to her view that goodness or the Good is the source of value, that which calls for our loving attention. Goodness should be loved because of its goodness, something does not become good because it is loved. And yet Murdoch writes: "The good artist, the true lover, the dedicated thinker, the unselfish moral agent … can

---

[24] Anscombe, "The First Person," 65.
[25] Chisholm, *Person and Object*, 15–52.

create the object of love. The dog's tooth, when sincerely venerated, glows with light" (1993: 506, 468).

We will not claim that *everything* Murdoch wrote is self-consistent or not in some kind of tension. After all, her identifying herself as a Platonist and a naturalist would seem contradictory to many philosophers.[26] Still, we offer three replies.

First, while we interpret Murdoch as a realist (there really are persons, things, and events that are good, independent of our desires and will), she believed *the idea* of goodness or the Good is created or invented, often by those devoted lovingly to honoring the goods that can transform our lives. On this point, Murdoch is not following the historical Plato, who sees the Good as an eternal form. She is following Plato insofar as Plato thought the form of the good takes time to grasp, but then Plato attributes creative, generative power to the good:

> In the region of the known the last thing to be seen and hardly seen is the idea of the good, and that when seen it must needs point us to the conclusion that this is indeed the cause of all that is right and beautiful, giving birth in the visible world to light, and the author of light and itself in the intelligible world being the authentic source of truth and reason, and that anyone who is to act wisely in private or public must have caught sight of this.[27]

We read Murdoch as claiming that we come to realize the reality of the Good and its essential being, but for Murdoch the Good is something we realize, rather than a preexisting form that creates all that is right and beautiful.

Second, the passage from Murdoch we cited continues with this sentence: "Compare, God *cannot* be thought of except as real" (1993: 506). She is here commenting on the ontological argument for the existence of God, which we take up in Section 5. Her view of the argument is complex, but at least one goal of her treatment is that, just as advocates of the argument cannot picture or envision God not existing, we seem to be in an analogous position of not being able to see the good as not existing. At least in the context of human life, Murdoch sees goodness and the Good as essential and necessary. In the passage cited about the Buddhist relic, perhaps she is observing how loving something may make us more open to recognizing what is real and sacred. Despite the son's deception, there may nonetheless be a good or sacred bond between the devout mother and the

---

[26] Gerson, *Platonism and Naturalism.*
[27] Republic, VII, 517 b–c.

well-meaning, wily son. Perhaps Murdoch's point is that, from a Buddhist perspective, Buddha-nature is in everything; we just have to attend to it in the right way.

Three, there is the common experience of the way love can increase goodness. So, in a friendship between persons (Chris and Pat), it would be odd to think that the love of one for the other creates the value of the other (the reason why Pat has value is because Chris loves Pat), but it is not at all odd to think that their *friendship* increases in value the more they love each other. Many of our relationships deepen or expand in value the more time and energy or love we invest in such relationships. Returning to the case of the relic, a long history of persons going on pilgrimage to venerate a relic might generate and increase the loving relationships between individuals and communities in their common devotion.

Having offered some considerations that may mitigate the force of the Tibetan objection, readers may conclude her example does not fit in easily with her moral realism.[28] Murdoch herself had reservations about putting a premium on coherence: "The achievement of coherence is itself ambiguous. Coherence is not necessarily good, and one must question its cost. Better sometimes to remain confused" (1993: 146–147).

Be that as it may, we end this section by citing a passage from *The Sovereignty of Good* in which Murdoch identified the Good as a concept and a worthy object to pursue in our world of imperfection and frailty. The Good is to be sought and loved. Perfect goodness may not be reached in this world, but it is a real goal to be sought. Murdoch wrote:

> Good is a concept about which, and not only in philosophical language, we naturally use a Platonic terminology, when we speak about seeking the Good, or loving the Good. We also may speak seriously of ordinary things, people, works of art, as being good, although we are also well aware of their imperfections. Good lives as it were on both sides of the barrier and we can combine the aspiration to complete goodness with a realistic sense of achievement within our limitations. For all our frailty the command 'be perfect' has sense for us. The concept Good resists collapse into the selfish empirical consciousness. It is not a mere value tag of the choosing will, and functional and causal uses of 'good' (a good knife, a good fellow) are not, as some philosophers have wished to argue, clues to the structure of the concept. The proper and serious use of the term refers us to a perfection which perhaps is not exemplified in the world we know. (1970: 90–91)

---

[28] As claimed by Alan Jacobs in "G(o)od in Iris Murdoch."

3.3 Life as Pilgrimage

Despite Murdoch's claim that human life has no *telos* or purpose or justification from an external point of view, she did articulate what may be described as a life well lived. This is a life in which we move increasingly to revere and respond to the myriad of goods revealed by our loving attention. A preeminent example is in a loving relationship between persons. For Murdoch, persons are so complex and many-layered that the task of knowing and loving another person is virtually an inexhaustible, ongoing task, sometimes generating happiness and fulfillment, but also fraught with danger. Life can be a pilgrimage or quest as we are transformed by our love of the Good, but it can also be a disastrous failure to escape our ego-serving fantasies.

Murdoch disparaged the modern twentieth-century hero and anti-hero in Western literature, the lone hero, existing as an isolated will:

> We know this novel and its hero well. The story of the lonely brave man, defiant without optimism, proud without pretension, always an exposer of shams, whose mode of being is a deep criticism of society. He is an adventurer. He is godless ... (D. H. Lawrence, E. Hemingway, A. Camus, J. P. Sartre, K. Amis) ... His will, that adventurous instrument that makes him so different from sticks and stones and billiard balls and greengrocers and bank managers, his will is separate from the rest of his being and uncontaminated. He *might* do anything. (1997: 225)

Murdoch found great fault with a will that is driven to power as life's meaning and goal. She was also critical of the philosophical position of her time concerning the will's role in morality and ethics, which we have outlined earlier. By way of contrast, she believed that the pilgrimage one must take is to become more virtuous, "... nothing in life is of any value except the attempt to be virtuous" (1970: 85) through attention to what is outside of oneself, especially other people. It is an attention to what transcends self, but without a transcendent source of help found in religious traditions that picture God, or gods, as personal and the source of power for change.

But how is this Murdochian effort of the individual learning how to pay attention in order to become a better person radically different from the lone hero of Nietzsche and those thinkers who inherited his notion of "the will"? You could say the difference lies in the goal; the will to power is a different goal than the goal of becoming more virtuous by pursuing the Good. But Murdoch's picture of the individual is still somewhat analogous to the heroic model she rejects. In her portrayals, individuals still struggle, often in isolation, in a godless universe. "God sees us and seeks us – the Good does not" (1993: 83).

Murdoch draws on Plato's *Anamnesis*, spiritual memory, that belongs to the individual who "remembers" pure forms of goodness and beauty with which he was familiarly "face to face" ("not in a glass darkly") in another existence (1993: 23). For Plato this is a divine dispensation of "grace." In his book *The Sleeping Beauty and Other Essays*, the American scholar Ralph Harper uses the fairy tale of Sleeping Beauty to narrate the experience of nostalgia or homesickness as an unwilled, or unbidden, emotion that reminds one of a wholeness lost that might be regained. Murdoch says of another writer, Proust, that his illuminations are "involuntary, gifts from the gods, not experiences or states which could be attained or prolonged by a (morally, spiritually) disciplined way of living" (1993: 263). She looks again to Plato to adopt his "slow shift of attachments wherein looking (concentrating, attending, attentive discipline) is a source of divine (purified) energy" (1993: 25). In her eagerness to be better, Murdoch asks why we must wait for grace or unbidden emotion to become better, more whole. "Why do we have to wait for accidental inspirational experiences which may, if we are lucky, make us artists? Should we not attempt to turn most of our time from dead (inattentive, obsessed, etc.) time into live time?" (1993: 263). Should this sound overly optimistic as a self-improvement project, Murdoch never says that an individual will be successful in continuously moving ever upward to the Good, but she places the attempt to move closer to the Good as a virtue at the very top of the list.

In her play *Above the Gods,* Murdoch has Plato claim:

> In a way, goodness and truth seem to come out of the depths of the soul, and when we really know something we feel we've always known it. Yet also it's terribly distant, farther than any star. We're sort of – stretched out – It's like beyond the world, not in the clouds or heaven, but a light that *shows* the world, this world, as it really is. (1993: 518)

We will revisit this matter in Sections 4 and 5 of this Element.

We conclude this section with three further observations, beginning with a clarification. Some of Murdoch's language may suggest that she thinks of life as pointless and without purpose. "The Good has nothing to do with purpose, indeed it excludes the idea of purpose" (1970: 69, 85). This sounds a little like Sartre's declaration at the end of *Being and Nothingness:* "man is a useless passion."

We suggest Murdoch, unlike Sartre, was underscoring the intrinsic value of virtue and goodness; one is not to pursue virtue and goodness for the sake of reward by God or karmic law or even for the sake of happiness. In this spirit, one might say that a good friendship is pointless, to dramatically insist that the value of the friendship is not for the sake of career advancement, financial enrichment, self-pleasure, and so on. So, Murdoch might say that some goods lack a use or some further purpose, while not saying they are useless, insofar as that suggests they are of no value whatever and utterly dispensable. Moreover, Murdoch's notion of pilgrimage could not be further from Sartre's main character in his novel *Nausea:* Roquentin claimed that he had never had an adventure; there were no adventures. Murdoch extolled philosophical pilgrimage – which had a goal – and wrote novels in which some potential pilgrimages turn out to be misadventures. In her novel *The Severed Head*, adultery and betrayal are ruinous to characters who might have been good pilgrims.

Second, Murdoch lamented the ways in which psychoanalysis and the diminished practice of religion have fed our sense of living in a world without values. She counters that, in practice, psychoanalytic therapy is wedded to a host of its own values and evaluations. Moreover, she proposed that our retreat from valuing what used to be called the soul is a failure on our part; a failure of love and eros:

> In practice psychoanalytical therapy, as treatment of human individuals with histories, cannot avoid being involved in moral judgement, in moral reflection and insight in the widest sense. This moral aspect of their work is now recognized in the claim of some practitioners that all analysis is lay analysis. It is the soul that is being treated. The notion that the soul can, in its travail, become the analysand of an authoritative science contributes to an atmosphere wherein people resolutely ignore moral and religious aspects of their *experience*. It has become unfashionable, even among theologians and moralists to refer to such experience.... Absence of ritual from ordinary life also starves the imagination; institutions, schools, universities, even churches abandon it. But when we say that 'religion is disappearing' part of what is disappearing is both the occurrence of certain experiences, and also our tendency to *notice* them and, instinctively or reflectively, to lend them moral or religious meaning. A lack of Eros. (1993: 307)

We believe there is merit to Murdoch's account.

It is interesting that the term "soul" has not only endured but has also come to more notice in secular, therapeutic literature. For example, the secular (atheist) Oliver Sacks referred to the souls of his patients.[29] And on Murdoch's point about religion disappearing and with it certain experiences, we grant that this may be so in some parts of the world, but not

---

[29] Sacks, "The Lost Mariner," *The Man Who Mistook His Wife for a Hat*, 27–51.

others.[30] We add that contemporary philosophers and theologians are now much more sensitive to the affective, experiential dimension of religious life, its eros, our loves and hopes.[31]

3.4 Transcending a Binary View of Gender

Murdoch's work may be seen as transcending the binary view of there being a profound, essential dichotomy between males and females. In an interview, she shared her personal view of men and women:

> I identify with men more than women, I think. I don't think it's a great leap; there's not much of a difference, really. One's just a human being. I think I'm more interested in men than women. I'm not interested in women's problems as such, though I'm a great supporter of women's liberation – particularly education for women – but in aid of getting women to join the human race, not in aid of making any kind of feminine contribution to the world. I think there's a kind of human contribution, but I don't think there's a feminine contribution.[32]

Murdoch was keenly aware of the ways sexism harms women. In the first section, we cited Mary Midgley and how she, Murdoch, and their female friends found the male-centric atmosphere at Oxford University stultifying. On sexism, Murdoch observed:

> The notion that women are inferior is deep, very deep, even in our fairly sensible society, and it does nobody any good. Men and women are still thought of as having stereotyped parts to play, regardless of their temperament. But any individual is a mixture of masculine and feminine and would be best employed just being himself and treating people as individuals, too.[33]

True, in this passage, Murdoch retains a conceptual distinction between masculine and feminine (or she recognizes that such stereotypes exist), but her ideal vision is one of freedom from such categories as essential features, so that biological females need not adopt an exclusively feminine identity, and similarly with males.

Murdoch's novels reveal a great deal of her exploration of gender roles. Her novels include characters with a wide spectrum of sexual and gender identities, including transsexuality and what today is called "gender fluidity." Several of her novels have male narrators, and plots move easily

---

[30] Taliaferro, *Religions: A Quick Immersion.*
[31] Taliaferro and Evans, *Is God Invisible?*
[32] Dooley (ed.), *From a Tiny Corner in the House of Fiction,* 48.
[33] Dooley (ed.), *From a Tiny Corner in the House of Fiction,* 5.

among male, female, and sexually ambiguous events. For a good guide, see *The Saint and the Artist: A Study of the Fiction of Iris Murdoch*, by Peter J. Conradi.[34]

We are not presenting an argument here in support of Murdoch's philosophy of gender, but we are identifying Murdoch's resistance to essentialist views of gender. She believed we as individuals should not see ourselves as determined by socially defined gender roles.

We now turn to Murdoch's aesthetics.

4 Beauty, Truth, and Good Art

> Art and morals are ... one. Their essence is the same. The essence of both of them is love. Love is the perception of individuals. Love is the extremely difficult realization that something other than oneself is real. Love, and so art and morals, is the discovery of reality. What stuns us into realization of our supersensible destiny is not, as Kant imagined, the formlessness of nature, but rather its unutterable particularity; and most particular and individual of all natural things is the mind of men.
>
> Iris Murdoch (1997: xiv–xv)

So far in this Element, we have seen Murdoch develop her philosophy of the self and values by appealing to our conscious self-awareness and our experience of values, thereby overcoming the entrenched fact/value bifurcation that dominated her contemporary intellectual climate. Moving forward, Murdoch looked to the experience of beauty and art to ground her view of truth and enhance her theory of values.

We begin with Murdoch's reflections on the experience of beauty in the natural world.

4.1 Unselfish Love and Beauty

According to Murdoch, the experience of beauty can play a vital role in freeing our psyches from self-preoccupation and fantasies. Her appeal to experience is very much in keeping with her trusting that experience will present insights into how to think about things. These insights, in turn, can be tested in light of experience:

> I am looking out of my window in an anxious and resentful state of mind, oblivious of my surroundings, brooding perhaps on some damage done to my prestige. Then suddenly I observe a hovering kestrel. In a moment everything is altered. The brooding self with its hurt vanity has disappeared. There is nothing now but kestrel. And when I return to thinking of the other matter it seems less important. (1970: 82)

---

[34] Bolton, "Murdoch and Feminism," 438–450.

The encounter with the beautiful movement of the kestrel is an arrest of the whole person; what Murdoch calls "unselfing." This experience of self-forgetting and being immersed in a moment out-of-time is an altered state of mind. Its impact is to shift the balance of her former preoccupations, helping dissipate the intense negative emotions of resentment and anxiety.

Experiences of beauty inaugurate "unselfing" and Murdoch reminds us that Plato observed "beauty is the only spiritual thing which we love by instinct" (1970: 83). And it is the particular things that we love that Murdoch calls on to demonstrate that this is not an abstract concept or theory. We know that in our own experiences of beauty we forget ourselves, if even momentarily. This is why her retelling of the moment with the kestrel is so moving. We are looking out the window with her and we hover with the kestrel too.

Murdoch's understanding of beauty, like Plato's in the Symposium, involves love as eros. From a Platonist perspective, we are driven by eros or desire, either for that which is truly good or bad. Ideally, our pilgrimage should lead us toward the Good, the beautiful reality that, for Murdoch, outshines traditional notions of God. While a Christian Platonist might hold that the beauty in the world reflects and participates in the beauty of God, a Murdochian Platonist considers how experiences of beauty lead to a greater love and devotion to the Good.

In the following passage, Murdoch appreciates how eros is a powerful force that can lead us to the true and good or to error and destitution.

> 'Eros' is the continuous operation of spiritual *energy*, desire, intellect, love, as it moves among and responds to particular objects of attention, the force of magnetism and attraction which joins us to the world, making it a better or worse world: good and bad desires with good and bad objects. It gives sense to the idea of loving good, something absolute and unique, a magnetic focus, made evident in our experience through innumerable movements of cognition. Good represents the reality of which God is the dream. It purifies the desire which seeks it. This is not just a picturesque metaphysical notion. People speak of loving all sorts of things, their work, a book, a potted plant, a formation of clouds. Desire for what is corrupt and worthless, the degradation of love, its metamorphosis into ambition, vanity, cruelty, greed, jealousy, hatred, or the parched demoralizing deserts of its absence, are phenomena often experienced and readily recognised. If we summon up a great energy, it may prove to be a great demon. People know the difference between good and evil, it takes quite a lot of theorizing to persuade them to say or imagine that they do not. The activity of Eros is orientation of desire. Reflecting in these ways we see 'salvation' or 'good' as connected with, or incarnate in, all sorts of particulars, and not just an 'abstract idea.'

> 'Saving the phenomena' is happening all the time. We do not lose the particular, it teaches us love, we understand it, we *see* it, as Plato's carpenter sees the table, or Cézanne sees Mont Ste Victoire or the girl in the bed-sitter sees her potted plant or her cat. (1993: 496–497)

Murdoch's devotion to the aesthetics of particular things led her to differ from a common interpretation of Plato's teaching (through the figure Diotima in the Symposium). In that teaching, we are instructed to ascend a ladder, beginning with loving particular things and ascending to greater beauty, leaving the lesser beauties behind. In Murdoch's vision, the experience of different beauties might be pictured as a fountain in which there is a continuous, cyclical flow of water. In this image, the "lesser beauties" are not left behind, but are part of a continuous, flowing experience. In this metaphor of a fountain, beauty begets beauty.

Murdoch's affirmation of a realist view of beauty was part of a restoration of beauty as a serious philosophical topic. The title of Mary Mothersill's 1987 book was well-chosen: *Beauty Restored*. Two other champions in restoring beauty were Guy Sircello and Elaine Scary.

Murdoch's alignment of beauty and goodness raises a well-known objection. Aren't there cases of what appears to be beautiful that are actually morally repugnant? Examples range from Leni Riefenstahl's 1935 Nazi propaganda film *The Triumph of the Will*, to the ostensible beauty of a mushroom cloud arising from nuclear destruction of a city, to the aesthetically arresting details of photographs of great violence. Granted most are cases such as Murdoch's attention to the kestrel, but isn't the experience of beauty sometimes a catalyst for abhorrent emotions and action?

We suggest that the alleged counter-examples lose their aesthetic appeal (or their entitlement to being considered authentic beauty) when their aesthetic appeal is placed fully in context.[35] Granted, Riefenstahl's film has inventive aesthetic features (drama, momentum, distorted perspectives, effective lighting, and music). But when the film is assessed in light of the genocide committed by the Nazi German regime, it becomes revolting and an object worthy of abhorrence, a work in which murderers are portrayed as innocent agents of justice. The mushroom cloud may be seen as having a pleasant, organic, sensual shape, but cannot reasonably be experienced as beautiful by someone who takes seriously the incineration of thousands of people, some who survived and suffered injuries for life. A similar

---

[35] For a detailed discussion and analysis of Murdoch's connection between goodness and truthfulness in art, see Rudd, *Painting and Presence*.

response can be fashioned about the photographs. However aesthetically intriguing the color red appears in a photographic composition, its appeal is expunged when it is understood that the red is blood flowing from a victim of violence.

For a further defense of a realist view of beauty, we refer you to two of our books.[36]

4.2 The Power of Art

Murdoch is among the few well-known artists in Western-European culture (including Leo Tolstoy and Wassily Kandinsky) to contribute to the field of philosophy of art. Her love of art long preceded her first novel, published in 1954. Her passion for stories grew out of a rich exposure in her childhood; her parents introduced her to all kinds of literature: novels, history, adventure, poetry, biography, and Shakespeare. Her boarding school, Badminton School, included the arts in its curriculum, and Murdoch was remembered as being "interested and gifted at art."[37]

A brief overview of her aesthetics: Murdoch thought that art plays a valuable and consequential role in shaping our understanding of ourselves in the world. Works of art may also expand and shape our identity. Ideally, the making and experience of great art can strengthen our resistance to materialism and reductionism. It can aid us in energizing our self-purifying pilgrimage by integrating our emotions and intellect. All this serves our desire to seek the truth and to do so in cooperation with artists. Her ambitious position(s) distinguish her work from a famous 1951 essay titled "The Dreariness of Aesthetics," by John Passmore. In that essay, Passmore complained that the field of aesthetics was dull due to its preoccupation with abstract theory and its failure to engage concrete cases and experiences of art. There was nothing bleak or dreary about Murdoch's aesthetics.

On the importance of art discovering or giving form to our experience, Murdoch wrote:

> So in a way as word-users we all exist in a literary atmosphere, we live and breathe literature, we are all literary artists, we are constantly employing language to make interesting forms out of experience which perhaps originally seemed dull or incoherent. How far reshaping involves offenses against truth is a problem any artist must face. A deep motive for making literature or art of any sort is the desire to defeat the formlessness of the world and cheer oneself up by constructing forms out of what otherwise seems a mass of senseless rubble. (1997: 6–7)

---

[36] Taliaferro and Evans, *The Image in Mind* and *Is God Invisible?*
[37] Conradi, *Iris Murdoch: A Life*, 74.

Murdoch's appreciation for art guides us through an ever-widening circle of goods that ultimately wraps the artwork together with, to use Murdoch's term, "the client." These goods are realized through the concentration of the artwork acting on the concentration of the client, what Murdoch called a "sustained experienced mental synthesis" (1993: 3). She continued:

> Art is informative and entertaining, it condenses and clarifies the world, directing attention to particular things. This intense showing, this bearing witness, of which it is capable is detested by tyrants who always persecute or demoralize their artists. Art illuminates accident and contingency and the general muddle of life, the limitations of time and the discursive intellect, so as to enable us to survey complex or horrible things which would otherwise appall us. It creates an authoritative public human world, a treasury of past experience, it preserves the past. Art makes places and opens spaces for reflection, it is a defense against materialism and against pseudo-scientific attitudes to life. It calms and invigorates, it gives us energy by unifying, possibly by purifying, our feelings. In enjoying great art we experience a clarification and concentration and perfection of our own consciousness. Emotion and intellect are unified into a limited whole. In this sense art also *creates* its client; it inspires intuitions of ideal formal and symbolic unity which enable us to co-operate with the artist and to be, as we enjoy the work, artists ourselves. (1993: 8)

We often think of works of art as material objects. We are inclined to point to a painting on a wall or a sculpture in the garden. Pinpointing the location of a novel, play, music, and poetry brings to the fore the question of where works of art are located. From Murdoch's perspective, a work of art, whether a painting or a poem, is a work in any number of forms (material or immaterial) created in a complex context of intentions and desires that can have an important relational life. In setting up the concept, Murdoch explained:

> A work of art is of course not a material object, though some works of art are bodied forth by material objects so as to seem to inhere in them. In the case of a statue the relation between material object and the art object seems close, in the case of a picture less so. Poems and symphonies are clearly not material objects.
> All art objects are 'performed' or imagined first by the artist and then by his clients, and these imaginative and intellectual activities or experiences may be said to be the point or essence of art. (1993: 2–3)

In this framework, the work of art is what is experienced in the mind of the client in attending to, giving over to, what has been performed or imagined by the artist.

For Murdoch, experiencing works of art can move us with inward pressure (by intense showing, bearing witness, purifying, unifying, and invigorating) toward a Platonic experience of transcendence, prompting illumination, reflection, joy, calm, or clarity. She proposes that works of art can have a private and public dimension; she depicts the way art functions inwardly for artist and recipient, while also recognizing works of art in the public arena, bringing people together.

Consistent with her moral philosophy and the role attention plays in pursuit of the Good, it is *attention* in her philosophy of art that dissolves any distance between the artwork and the attending person. This experiential unity is due to art's power to carry some new truth that resonates in the attentive mind, reminding us there is an underlying order and unity we have known, even if only in momentary instances.

The reciprocity Murdoch highlights between ourselves and the artist is the result of a call and response activity on the part of the artist and her medium, the medium whose limitations help provide the resistances that make transcendence a possibility. The artist transcends self in confronting the reality of other, be it material, the limits of language, the physics of color, sound, gravity, and so on.

This unity and reciprocity experienced by the artist and artwork is illustrated as occurring very naturally in an activity quite common to human beings, with evidence of it as early as the Paleolithic cave paintings at Altamira and Lascaux. In his book *Free Play: Improvisation in Life and Art*, Stephen Nachmanovitch describes how the painters used the three-dimensional surfaces of the cave walls:

> The positioning and attitudes of the animals were suggested, even necessitated, by the bulges, folds, crevices, and jagged textures of the rock walls on which they were made. Some of the power of these paintings resides in the way the painters were able to create mutual adaptation between the shapes of their spiritual imagination and the shapes of the hard rock.[38]

Nachmanovitch goes on to retell a passage out of the novel *A High Wind in Jamaica*, by Richard Hughes. A group of children are kidnapped by pirates on the high seas and one of them, a girl, is staring at the wood grain on the plank wall in the ship's cabin. She starts to see faces and shapes in the wood grain and begins to draw them, creating a scene. Nachmanovitch retells:

> When the child completes the gestalt of the wood grain, there is an encounter between the patterns given in the seemingly random swirls

---

[38] Nachmanovitch, *Free Play*, 85.

of wood grain residing outside the child and the patterns given by the child's inner nature. The wood grain (or tree, or rock, or cloud) *educes*, or draws out of the child, something related to what the child knows, but that is also more or different than what the child knows because the child is both assimilating the outside pattern to her desires and accommodating herself to the outside pattern … This is the eternal dialogue between making and sensing.[39]

Nachmanovitch draws on this story to shed light on the reciprocal nature of artmaking between the inner life of the artist and the material(s) chosen and how they inform each other.

For Murdoch, this "eternal dialogue between making and sensing" is pulled and guided by the magnetism of the Good, for artists and for all of us. Murdoch focused on the aesthetic dimension of our experience in the world to illustrate the importance of unselfing in developing moral understanding and maturity. Contemplation of even the smallest details and particulars of things brings awareness of values, that our perceptions are steeped in values. Murdoch wrote:

> A contemplative observation of contingent 'trivial' detail (insects, leaves, shapes of screwed up paper, looks and shadows of anything, expressions of faces) is a prevalent and usually, at least in a minimal sense, 'unselfing' activity of consciousness. This might also be called an argument from perception. It 'proves,' as against generalizing and reductionist philosophical or psychological theories, that consciousness or awareness can be spoken of in theoretical discussions of morality. It is a place where the moral and the aesthetic join. It marks a path through the aesthetic. (1993: 245)

When you contemplate the aesthetic dimension of anything, you move your attention to what exists outside of yourself, and that attention to what is "other" is part of your pilgrimage to the Good, which necessarily involves the moral life.

Though the imagination can go in any direction, the aesthetic, for Murdoch, is bound to the moral life through a Platonic understanding of "a slow shift of attachments wherein *looking* (concentrating, attending, attentive discipline) is a source of divine energy" (1993: 24–25). Linking the moral, the aesthetic, and the divine finds expression in her later writing when she speculated about the possibility of greatly expanding our definitions of what is religious, what is spiritual, which we take up in Section 5.

---

[39] Ibid., 86.

In the moral pilgrimage of attention, the work of the artist is to focus imagination in a very specific direction if great art is the goal, if anything great can be achieved. For Murdoch, "We use our imagination not to escape from reality but to join it" (1970: 88). Murdoch's understanding of the imagination stands in contrast to Freud's theories that art is wish fulfillment and a result of unconscious forces in the psyche. Murdoch was impressed with Freud's picture of the human condition and agreed with him that we are naturally selfish and lack objectivity. Freud's theories were heavily indebted to Plato, but she found his thinking about the mechanics of desire, will, and mental health to be reductive and enclosed (1997: 341–342). Murdoch's vision is one where self-transcendence, paradoxically perhaps, connects one's self to the real through attention. She saw art's task to pursue the real as its most liberating and profound gift to the world. Notice Murdoch's ambivalence about Freud. She thought he correctly saw our ego-driven energy, but was wrong about the source and potential liberating power of good art. She said:

> To know oneself *in the world* (as part of it, subject to it, connected with it) is to have the firmest grasp of the real. This is the humble 'sense of proportion' Plato connects with virtue. Strong agile realism, which is of course not photographic naturalism, the non-sentimental, non-meanly-personal imaginative grasp of the subject-matter is something which can be recognised as value in all the arts, and it this which gives that special unillusioned pleasure which is the liberating whiff of reality; when in high free play the clarified imaginative attention of the creative mind is fixed upon its object. Of course art is playful, but its play is serious. (1997: 459)

Murdoch extolled the emancipatory potential of art:

> The art object conveys, in the most accessible and for many the only available form, the idea of a transcendent perfection. Great art inspires because it is separate, it is for nothing, it is for itself. It is an image of virtue. Its condensed, clarified presentation enables us to look without sin upon a sinful world. It renders innocent and transforms into truthful vision our baser energies connected with power, curiosity, envy, and sex. (1993: 8)

This is an extraordinarily high view of the power of great art.

4.3 Truth and Fantasy

Murdoch's view of the imagination is indebted to Coleridge and his distinction between fancy (for Murdoch "fantasy") and imagination (1993: 209). Imagination is a creative faculty that works in depth to create unity and wholeness, to reveal and to explain. When fantasy shapes the artwork, it "operates either with shapeless daydreams ... or with small myths, toys, crystals. Each in his own way produces a sort of 'dream necessity.' Neither grapples with reality: hence 'fantasy,' not imagination" (1997: 292).

Murdoch was relentless in insisting that the imagination must be engaged in seeking truth, and good art is the fruit of this search:

> I think good art is good for people precisely because it is not fantasy but imagination. It breaks the grip of our dull fantasy life and stirs us to the effort of true vision. Most of the time we fail to see the big wide real world at all because we are blinded by obsession, anxiety, envy, resentment, fear. (1997: 14)

Murdoch did not view the imagination as separate from morality or morally neutral. "Imagination is a mixed matter.... It is an intelligent sensibility; it can feel about in the dark and move both sides of the barriers" (1993: 310). She took imagination to be inseparable from thinking itself. She held that when we "settle down to be 'thoroughly rational' about a situation, we have already, reflectively or unreflectively, imagined it a certain way. Our deepest imaginings which structure the world in which 'moral judgments' occur are already evaluations. Perception itself is a mode of evaluation" (1993: 314–315).

As we have seen, a key question in Murdoch's moral philosophy is "How can I make myself better?" She was not satisfied with Kant's man, or Kantian man-god whose psyche is portrayed as demonic on the one hand and angelic on the other, all guided by the will to action. As part of her critique of Kant and the existentialists, she draws on her appreciation of Simone Weil's moral philosophy:

> We are not isolated free choosers, monarchs of all we survey, but benighted creatures sunk in a reality whose nature we are constantly and overwhelmingly tempted to deform by fantasy. Our current picture of freedom encourages a dream-like facility; whereas what we require is a renewed sense of the difficulty and complexity of the moral life and the opacity of persons.... Simone Weil said that morality was a matter of attention, not of will. We need a new vocabulary of attention. It is here that literature is so important, especially since it has taken over some of the tasks formerly performed by philosophy. Through literature we can re-discover a sense of the density of our lives. (1997: 293–294)

Eloquence in literature has innumerable expressions and Murdoch equated it with the attempt to speak the truth (1997: 294). The role of the imagination to reveal the truth of other persons was central to Murdoch's views on literature, and she frequently drew examples from Western literature of the nineteenth and twentieth centuries to explore how the individual is treated. She explored the differences between narratives, noting a large shift in the portrayal of the individual as part of a larger social structure in the nineteenth century to the isolated self in the twentieth century, poised as alone in need of defense against institutions and society, as we noted earlier. In tracing the isolation of the individual in existentialist literature, particularly of Sartre and Camus, she thought the vision was not true to our real interdependence. It did not reflect the moral imperative to recognize the reality of other persons.

Murdoch enlists Plato in discussing how the imagination works to reveal truth. She draws on the mythical God in the Timaeus portrayal as a "restless imaginative creative artist." Imagination is "a power working at the barrier of darkness, recovering verities which we somehow know of, but have in our egotistic fantasy life forgotten" (1993: 320).

In her essay "The Fire and the Sun," Murdoch traces Plato's view of the arts and artists through his dialogues and his attempts to link the eternal Forms with our world of contingencies, chance, and sensible experience. In the Timaeus, Plato introduces the Demiurge, an artist creator. The Demiurge is part of Plato's trinity of the Good, the Demiurge (creator), and the World Soul. The Good is changeless, eternal; the Demiurge is active, a moving force; and the World Soul is the incarnate spirit in the world of the senses.

In this image, Plato is able to provide a positive energy for creation that brings embodiment (the World Soul) with our ability to know something of the Forms through our experience of beauty, but it is an activity fraught with failure and imperfections, and even danger. Art can distract us from knowing the purity of truth.

Murdoch acknowledged Plato's hostility to the arts in many of her essays. She strove to reconcile this by reading Plato's hostility as evidence that he understood the potential power of art to lead one astray into fantasy and away from the truth. This reading provides a path for Murdoch to bring her love for Plato together with her love of great art and its potential to be part of the virtuous life:

> Good art, thought of as symbolic force rather than a statement, provides a stirring image of a pure transcendent value, a steady visible enduring good, and perhaps provides for many people, in an unreligious age without prayer or sacraments, their clearest *experience* of something grasped as separate and precious and beneficial and held quietly and unpossessively in the attention. Good art which we love can seem holy and attending to it can be like praying. Our relation to such art though

'probably never' entirely pure is markedly unselfish. The calm joy in the picture gallery is quite unlike the pleasurable flutter felt in the saleroom. Beauty is, as Plato says, visibly transcendent, hence indeed the metaphor of vision so indispensable in discussions of aesthetics and morality. (1997: 453)

Murdoch's final move to enjoin Plato with her high view of art comes at the end of the essay when she concluded:

> Plato is a great artist. It is not perhaps to be imagined that the paradox *(his views of art and his own writing)*, troubled him too much. Scholars in the land of posterity assemble the work and invent the problems. Plato had other troubles, many of them political. He fought a long battle against sophistry and magic, yet he produced some of the most memorable images in European philosophy: the cave, the charioteer, the cunning homeless Eros, the Demiurge cutting the Anima Mundi into strips and stretching it out crosswise. He kept emphasizing the imageless remoteness of the Good, yet kept returning in his exposition to the most elaborate uses of art. The dialogue form itself is artful and indirect and abounds in ironical and playful devices. (1997: 462)

4.4 Good and Bad Art

Murdoch refers to good and bad art and consistently holds that good art is rare. She promoted art that revealed the mysterious, the complex, and the deeply considered. Murdoch judges great art as revealing truths about what is real, its task is to take on and communicate what is true about whatever subject matter the artist is concerned with. She did not, however, have a formula or criteria of what that might look like or what form that might take. She held it could be sophisticated or unsophisticated, complicated or simple, traditional or breaking with tradition (1993: 314). She cautioned against having a predetermined idea about what form an artwork might take:

> What is called 'anti-art' is not a novel phenomenon. The latest art has often seemed like an anti-art and been so regarded by its friends as well as its enemies. At regular intervals in history the artist has tended to be a revolutionary or at least an instrument of change in so far as he has tended to be a sensitive and independent thinker with a job that is a little outside established society. (1997: 235)

She is confident that what we attentively love can offer some initial guidance: "One cannot feel unmixed love for a mediocre moral standard any more than one can for the work of a mediocre artist" (1970: 60).

Murdoch's understanding of the creative process gives us a definition of "rules" that most artists would agree reveals tremendous insight and knowledge of the creative process. She articulated the experience of creativity when an artist decides to make something, whether that is a painting, dance, poem, musical score, or highly conceptual work, all involve pursuing a question or a curious attraction to something seen, felt, heard, or thought. She wrote:

> The art object too must accord with rules, that is to have form, but here, in the creation of good art, the rules are not general rules, but rules invented in and for the making of the individual object itself. The object asserts and establishes its own method of *verification*. We demand *truth* from art, and great works of art refine and extend our conception and grasp of truth. Genius *invents* its own rules or modes, and good art as it moves toward this level may be partly judged in terms of this ability. Bad or mediocre art is clearly seen to be *obeying* 'general rules' or familiar formulae. (1993: 313)

Her noting that the "object asserts and establishes its own method of verification" is experienced by artists when they are guided by a goal of perfection, understood by Murdoch to be a means of measurement: How do I evaluate the goodness of what I have made? Artists often have the experience of thinking they are going to accomplish one thing, when in the process of making the art object, one experiences resistance. This can be through the materials (if it is a material artwork) or through a narrative, when, for example, a character in a novel does something that the writer is not expecting and may not even want the character to do. Some transcendent authority is asserting itself through the process of attending to the world being made that demands acknowledgment and solutions, if the work is not to be a work of pure fantasy or convention:

> The idea of perfection is a natural producer of order. In its *light* we come to see that A, which superficially resembles B, is really better than B.... This is the true sense of the 'indefinability' of the good, which was given a vulgar sense by Moore and his followers. It lies beyond, and it is from this beyond that it exercises its *authority* ... and it is in the work of artists that we see the operation most clearly. The true artist is obedient to the conception of perfection to which his work is constantly related and re-related in what seems an external manner. (1997: 350)

In *Salvation by Words*, she said, "all good art is its own intimate critic, celebrating in simple and truthful utterance the broken nature of its formal quality" (1997: 240). Artists can experience this in the form of taking up the brush again, on to the next work still driven to pursue because "I didn't quite get it yet; I thought I did, but there, I did not." Murdoch firmly believed that the importance of a work of art lay in its attempt to create a formal unity and complete statement (1997: 240).

While Murdoch did not prescribe any formula or program for what artists should pursue, other than to pursue getting outside one's ego and fantasies, she did have a hierarchy for literary forms, perhaps due to her own life's work as a novelist. What she wanted literature to put first: other people. She thought tragedy was the highest form of literature because it was the form that reveals a most profound truth. "All good tragedy is anti-tragedy. *King Lear*. Lear wants to enact the false tragic, the solemn, the complete. Shakespeare forces him to enact the true tragic, the absurd, the incomplete" (1997: 240).

Of all the art forms, she especially aligns literature with morality.

> It is important to remember that language itself is a moral medium, almost all uses of language convey value. This is one reason why we are almost always morally active. Life is soaked in the moral, literature is soaked in the moral. If we even attempt to describe this room our descriptions would naturally carry all sorts of values. Value is only artificially and with difficulty expelled from language for scientific purposes. So, the novelist is revealing his values by any sort of writing which he may do. He is particularly bound to make moral judgements in so far as his subject matter is the behavior of human beings. (1997: 27)

Her high view of great art is brought into focus further when she writes about the power and spiritual nature of language:

> Great art, then, by introducing a chaste self-critical precision into its mimesis, its representation of the world by would-be complete, yet incomplete, forms, inspires truthfulness and humility. (So Plato was partly right and partly wrong.) Great art is able to display and discuss the central area of our reality, our actual consciousness, in a more exact way than science or even philosophy can. I want to speak finally about one of the main tools of this exploration: words ... there is no doubt which art is the most practically important for our survival and our salvation, and that is literature. Words constitute the ultimate texture and stuff of our moral being, since they are the most refined and delicate and detailed, as well as the most universally used and understood, of the symbolisms whereby we express ourselves into existence. We became spiritual animals when we became verbal animals. The *fundamental* distinctions can only be made in words. Words are spirit. Of course eloquence is no guarantee of goodness, and an inarticulate man can be virtuous. But the quality of a civilization depends on its ability to discern and reveal truth, and this depends on the scope and purity of its language. (1997: 240–241)

5 Transcendence and the Natural World

> The felt need for this [large] picture, or field of force is answered by metaphysics and religion.... This is not a matter of specialized isolated moments of moral choice, appearing in a continuum of non-moral activity. These moments and responses are occurring all the time.
>
> Iris Murdoch (1993: 297)

Murdoch speaks of a felt need for a broad metaphysical and religious vision that could further validate and sustain her claims about the constant call to respond to values. Are there one or more views of the transcendent that can provide this larger picture? Her recognition of this felt need is in tension with another, earlier claim in *The Sovereignty of Good:* "Our destiny can be examined but it cannot be justified or totally explained. We are simply here" (1970: 77). Such a surprisingly deflationary conclusion is hardly encouragement for thinking about a broader, explanatory transcendent framework, whether atheistic or theistic. It is rare to claim that such frameworks offer *complete justification* or *total explanations* (many Christian theists, for example, allow for gratuitous evil and chance events), but might they provide some greater, ultimate explanation for understanding why we are here? This section considers the prospects of a quest for such a greater, transcendent framework.

We begin by considering whether there is (or may be) a meaningful, transcendent God beyond the natural world. We suggest that Murdoch's treatment of St. Anselm's ontological argument for God's existence can be reconstructed to justify the belief in God based on the ostensible (apparent) experience of God. Murdoch draws on the work of the medieval philosopher Anselm of Canterbury (d. 1109) to frame and expand her views of goodness and the Good. In her treatment of Anselm, we suggest she has left the door open, ever so slightly, for a defense of theism. The next section asks whether a form of Platonism, more Platonic than Murdoch's Platonism, atheistic or theistic, may ground and enhance some of Murdoch's values.

5.1 Murdoch and a Personal God

Murdoch was committed to some form of naturalism that, at the very least, holds that there is no God, the omnipresent, all-good, supreme, purposive reality transcending the natural world. Her atheism amounts to her rejecting the traditional theistic vision in the Abrahamic faiths and in theistic forms of Hinduism, Sikhism, the Bahai, and traditional indigenous practices.

A brief note on terminology: The term "personal God," which Murdoch used on occasion (1993: 50), needs clarifying. In this context we will use the term for any view of God that describes God as knowing, acting, having purposes and intentions, love, desire, and so on – whether these terms are used univocally (to say "God loves," uses the term "love" with same meaning when we say "we love you") or by analogy (God's love is analogous or similar to our love for you). In this Element, "personal" does not suggest ownership (to think of God as beholden to persons sounds more like magic or idolatry than traditional religion); it is used in contrast to an impersonal view of God, such as Spinoza's. Traditional Christian theology includes the belief that the Godhead is not homogenous but is composed of the three persons: Father, Son, and Holy Spirit. In what follows, we address, not the Trinity itself, but the Christian teaching of the incarnation in which the second member of the Trinity becomes incarnate as Jesus of Nazareth, who is believed to be wholly God and wholly human. So, while Jesus is *Totus Deus* (wholly God), he is not *Totum Dei* (the whole of God).

Murdoch considered her atheism open to challenge and not obviously true (1970: 74). In fact, she thought that atheism is not a facile matter: "It is easy to *say* there is no God. It is not so easy to believe it and to draw the consequences" (1997: 226). She rejected the idea of contemporaries, like Ayer, who thought that theism is meaningless. "It is not senseless to believe in God" (1997: 80, 93). "Belief in God is one solution, where we picture God both as pure transcendent Goodness, and also as a personal good-making intelligence active here below" (1993: 50). Similarly, Murdoch did not seem to regard her form of naturalism as self-evident and impervious to objections. She wrote about adopting an "inconclusive, non-dogmatic naturalism" (1970: 43). We believe that her expansive naturalism is more reasonable than the scientifically reductive form of naturalism. But broad-minded naturalists, like Murdoch, face the task of accounting for how consciousness, moral and aesthetic values, and individuals who undertake a pilgrimage to the Good have emerged from an impersonal, mindless cosmos. Murdoch herself may have taken the view that there is no need for such an account. But some theistic philosophers contend that they do have an account, for they believe consciousness, goodness, beauty, and love have always existed in God and not emerged from a mindless, physical, and lifeless cosmos. Murdoch understood the appeal of the ontological argument, as it avoids the problem of emergence. It begins with God as maximally excellent or valuable, a supreme being who then becomes the source of created goods, the *fons divinus* (divine fountain). She said:

> The most familiar (western) concept which gathers all value together into itself and then redistributes it is the concept of God; and of this too it may be said that unless you have it in the picture from the start you

cannot get it in later by extraneous means.... The Ontological Proof, unlike other alleged proofs of God's existence, shows, indeed uses, an awareness of this. (1993: 57)

While Murdoch claimed that "we need a theology that can continue without God" (1993: 511), she nonetheless understood the appeal of theism: "I like and respect the high and orthodox emphasis upon divine transcendence" (1993: 453). "The charm, attraction, and in many ways deep effectiveness of faith in a personal God must constantly strike the critical or envious outsider" (1993: 81). Interestingly, Murdoch does not always describe herself as an outsider: "I grew up in Anglican Christianity, and I feel in a way I am still inside the Anglican Church."[40] The love of God in theistic traditions fits her Platonic view of proper love and desire: "It is the function of God to be a non-degradable erotic object" (1993: 83). She concludes *Metaphysics as a Guide to Morals* with citing Psalm 139, which affirms God's omnipresence:

> Whither shall I go from thy spirit, whither shall I flee from thy presence? If I ascend into heaven thou art there, if I make my bed in hell, behold thou art there. If I take the wings of the morning and dwell in the uttermost parts of the sea, even there shall thy hand lead me, and thy right hand shall hold me. (1993: 512)

While Murdoch was likely using these verses to evoke our awe in the omnipresence of goodness or the Good, the use of the pronouns "thou" and "thy" strongly resonates with a personal God.

Murdoch suggested personal theism may support one's moral vision. Belief in the "all-seeing eye of God" can impede the sense of isolation and heighten one's sense of responsibility for others (1993: 463). Belief in an all-good, personal God may enable one to more fully come to realize the extent of evils in the world. Murdoch suggested:

> If one does not believe in a personal God there is no 'problem' of evil, but there is the almost insuperable difficulty of looking properly at evil and human suffering. It is very difficult to concentrate attention upon suffering and sin, in others and in oneself, without falsifying the picture in some way while making it bearable. (1970: 71)

Perhaps Murdoch was proposing that attending to suffering and sin is easier for a believer in an omniscient God who knows the suffering and sin and has the power and love to bring good out of such calamities.[41] It is

---

[40] Hawkins, "Iris Murdoch: Atheist, but unapologetically Anglican," 1.
[41] Adams, *Horrendous Evils and the Goodness of God*.

possible that in the absence of believing in such an ideal divine observer and redeemer, we may be greatly tempted to distort the truth in our eagerness for consolation.

Murdoch suggested that in religious theism there is vindication of her desire to affirm every moment counts in our lives:

> As we cannot keep track of items, to say that every moment counts may seem absurd; or else like a profession of faith. God sees it all. The Psalmist clearly thought that every moment counted. Is that simply poetic or picturesque? The idea of detailed scrutiny and potential judgement of all states of mind is not the exclusive property of traditional religion. If we call it a religious way of looking, we may be said to extend the concept of religion. (1993: 260)

Indeed we may, but we do well to realize that we are extending (or secularizing) the view that each moment and thing is of significance because it is created and sustained by an all-good, transcendent being (Ephesians 5:15-17; Colossians 4:5; Romans 3:1).

So, why did Murdoch reject the idea that there is a personal God? We believe that her chief reason was that she believed there is no widely acceptable, good reason for believing in theism. "I can see no evidence to suggest that human life is not self-contained" (1970: 77). The absence of widespread, indisputable evidence for God leads to evidence (or at least the presumption) of the absence of God. Still, Murdoch admits that establishing there is no transcendent telos is as difficult to establish as the opposite. "That human life has no external point or telos is a view as difficult to argue as its opposite, and I shall simply assert it" (1970: 77).

We believe that in *Metaphysics as a Guide to Morals*, Murdoch lays the groundwork for an Anselmian defense of theism. She points the way for making the claim that for some persons theism may be evident. We offer positive reasons for a highly limited Murdochian justification of theism, and then reply to her objections as to why we should not, in the end, accept Anselmian personal theism.

5.2 An Anselmian Pilgrimage into Contingency and Necessary Existence

Before embarking with Anselm, let us step back. How might we approach thinking about whether our cosmos has some transcendent cause?

Most philosophers in the debate between theism (affirmation of a personal, transcendent God) and naturalism (the denial of such a God) assume abundant facts: Our cosmos is not utterly chaotic; there are stable laws of nature enabling the existence of stars and planets, including our own in which there is life. Whatever we are, we came into being and are thinking, feeling, active beings, capable of cooperation and conflict, love and violence, procreation and murder, reasoning and madness, and artistic creation and destruction. We don't begin thinking about ourselves, values, and meaning in a vacuum. It appears that we are in a cosmos of great danger and evil, yet sufficiently hospitable for us to encounter abundant goods. And, if Murdoch is right, we can exercise our capacity either to love and attend to the goods of this world or to become mired in self-satisfying, destructive delusions and fantasies.

Moving forward, one way to envisage inquiry into whether our cosmos has some transcendent cause and sustainer is to inquire: If what we know of the cosmos has such complexity and unity (*and its appearance of design or purpose*), is it reasonable to believe that it has a purposive ultimate explanation? Or is it more reasonable to believe its cause is nonpersonal (perhaps the outcome of chance and necessity, to use Murdoch's terms)? Or is it more reasonable still to withhold judgment and be agnostic?

In the eighteenth century, William Paley proposed what would become a famous theistic argument from analogy. Imagine you are wandering about and come across a watch. Perhaps you have never seen a watch before (imagine you relied on sundials). Wouldn't it seem quite sensible to believe there was a watchmaker? The watch's intricacy and ticking movement would make the hypothesis of a watchmaker evident.

Over time, with the help of Darwinian evolutionary biology, many philosophers have thought they could just as well account for the object found (the cosmos) without an intelligent designer.

It is not our aim to assess this debate here. (Though we note, parenthetically, that Darwinian evolution cannot account for the laws of physics that make evolution possible.) Nor will we advocate a change of analogy: Imagine you came across all twenty-six novels by Iris Murdoch, but had no knowledge of her or any other books. Wouldn't it be reasonable to believe they had one or more authors? Let's grant (if only for the sake of argument) that over infinite time, a nonpurposive agent (in the philosophical literature, the agent is a nonintentional, unreflective monkey) might type all of Murdoch's novels, line by line, in order.

Laying aside whether such bizarre hypotheses would ever be reasonable, common to these cases is contingency: Both watchmaker and author (or monkey) are not necessarily existing. Our cosmos might have been lifeless and thus without any beings to make artifacts of any kind.

The ontological argument is on a different footing. The ontological argument centers around the idea that God, as the unsurpassably great (maximal) being, necessarily exists. The argument (and many versions of the cosmological argument) focuses on God's unconditional existence. If there is a God, God was not caused to exist by another being or popped into existence from nothing. God's very being is essential such that God cannot but exist. God's nonexistence is impossible, whereas our nonexistence is possible. God's existence is not the kind of conditional necessity between contingent objects. So, it is *necessarily true* that if Tokyo is larger than New York City, then New York City is smaller than Tokyo, but neither Tokyo nor New York City necessarily exists. At one time, neither existed; whereas if there is a God, there is no time God did not exist.

In several publications, Murdoch appreciates the importance of the ontological argument and its concept of God's necessity. In her first book, *Sartre: Romantic Rationalist*, Murdoch describes one of Sartre's characters, Roquentin, in his book *Nausea*, seeking to evade the contingency of the cosmos. Murdoch described him aspiring to be God-like: "He wishes that he himself existed necessarily" (1987: 43). In *The Sovereignty of Good*, Murdoch wrote:

> I am assuming there is no plausible 'proof' of the existence of God except some form of the ontological proof, a 'proof' incidentally which must now take on an increased importance in theology as a result of the recent 'de-mythologizing'. (1970: 61)

The reference to demythologizing is to theological reinterpreting traditional beliefs in miracles, the incarnation, and even God. ("God" might turn out to be "being" or "an object of ultimate concern," rather than the creator.) Demythologizing was popular in theological debate in the 1960s. If the ontological argument succeeds, God's necessary existence would not be a myth. Murdoch was not unhappy with some myth-making and unmaking, but she first and foremost wanted to engage reality. If her atheism was false or misguided, she wanted to know.

We suggest that Murdoch's atheism hinges partly on the ontological argument *not* succeeding as evidence for theism. As noted earlier, Murdoch is famous for claiming that "we are simply here" (1970: 77). And if God is a contingent being, Murdoch's view seems equivalent to a theist claiming that "God is simply here." But if Anselm and other advocates of the ontological argument are right, then God exists necessarily; unlike ourselves and our cosmos, God is not contingent; God cannot but exist; God's very essence is existence. God is not simply here (or everywhere).[42] If this view of God as necessarily existing is coherent, isn't there reason to inquire whether there is a transcendent, necessarily existing, purposive reality that can account for the cosmos and be a source of meaning in our lives? In the *Philosophical Investigations*, Wittgenstein wrote, "Explanations come to an end somewhere."[43] If we know that there is nothing beyond our contingent natural world, let's limit explanations to this world. But if there may be a necessarily existing, transcendent, supremely good reality, why not consider this broader, metaphysical point of view?

There are many versions of the ontological argument. Roughly speaking, the Anselmian version Murdoch addresses could be put as follows: (1) The concept of God is the concept of a maximally great (unsurpassably excellent) being. (2) As such, God has the greatest compossible set of great-making properties ("compossible" means properties that may be simultaneously instantiated by the same subject or being). The properties include omnipotence, omniscience, unsurpassable goodness, and necessary existence. (3) Such a being exists necessarily or it is impossible for the being to exist. (4) It is possible such a being exists. (5) Therefore that being is not impossible and exists necessarily, viz., in reality.[44]

The argument (and all its variants) has been challenged on almost every front, but it has its defenders. The reasoning from something being possibly necessary to concluding it is necessary is less odd than it appears. Take an obvious truth ($1 + 1 = 2$) and an obvious falsehood ($1 + 1 = 3$). As mathematical propositions, they are not contingently true or false. The necessity of the first is entailed by the thesis that it is possible that $1 + 1 = 2$, whereas the impossibility of $1 + 1 = 3$ is entailed when one realizes it is not possible that $1 + 1 = 3$. These propositions are often analyzed as matters of identity, the reason $1 + 1 = 2$ is true is that the equation is understood to

---

[42] Like many defenders of Anselm's argument, we are relying on *Proslogion*, chapter three, where Anselm links the concept of God as that-than-which-a-greater-cannot-be-thought with the idea that God's nonexistence cannot be thought. The basic idea is that a perfect being would be one whose nonexistence is inconceivable. Arguably, the worship of God in theistic traditions would be inimicable to the idea that God is a mere accident or might not have existed or that there could have been a God even greater than the God who is worshipped. Medieval philosophers who favored Anselm's reasoning about God include William of Auxerre, Richard Fischacre, Alexander of Hales, Bonaventura, Matthew of Aquasparta, Nicolaus of Cusa, and Duns Scotus (see Hartshorne, 1965: 154, for a longer list).

[43] Wittgenstein, *Philosophical Investigations*, 1.

[44] For recent constructive work on the ontological argument, see Nagasawa, *Maximal God* and Leftow, *Anselm's Argument*. We also recommend an earlier book, Charles Hartshorne's *Anselm's Discovery*.

be 1 + 1 is the same as 1 + 1. But, as Murdoch appreciates, pondering the existence of the God of Christian faith is not akin to such abstract objects.

In her treatment of Anselm's work, Murdoch makes three constructive contributions: She contends that Anselm's God is personal (which is sometimes denied); she elucidates the idea of God existing necessarily; she places the stages of the argument in the context of Anselm's ostensible experience of God's presence, which suggests that premises 1 to 4 may be supported by religious experience; she contends that some of the standard objections to the argument fail. Let's consider each of these.

The personal God of Anselm: Some philosophers deny that the God of the Bible and of Christian philosophers like Anselm and Aquinas is a person. Brian Davies writes: "The formula 'God is a person' does not occur in the Bible. Nor, so far as I know, is it present in the writings of any Christian theologians from New Testament times to the end of the Middle Ages."[45] In the following passage Davies references Aquinas, but he might just as well refer to Anselm:

> Persons are presumably human beings – animals with a particular way of functioning, things that learn and develop, things that talk and go through reasoning processes, things existing in a world of space and time, things that come to be and pass away, things [Aquinas would say] that depend for their being on God. That God [the divine nature] is one of *those* things is not a suggestion Aquinas could take seriously since, given his approach to creation, it looks as though it is assimilating God to a creature of some kind.[46]

If the above represents a definition of what it is to be a person, perhaps Davies has a point.

While we shall see later in this section that Murdoch does take issue with the anthropomorphic nature of a personal God, she seems to be on solid ground when she claims: "Anselm believed in a personal God, the God of Abraham, Isaac and Jacob, with whom the Psalter held converse. Anselm prayed to this Person, talked with him and experienced his personal presence" (1993: 401). Davies is working with the idea that a person must be a contingent, finite animal. In the writings of Anselm, it is overwhelmingly obvious that when he talks to God, he does not think he is addressing a finite, contingent, created thing, perhaps a powerful vertebrate or some impersonal force. The personal nature of Anselm's God is made evident when Anselm addresses God as "you" as in: "Grant me the knowledge

---

[45] Davies, "Simplicity," 38.
[46] Ibid.

that you exist just as we believe, and that you are what we believe."[47] The term "person" may not appear in the Bible, but wouldn't it be baffling if we were to regard all the figures in the Bible (from Adam and Eve to Jesus and the disciples) as nonpersons? The Bible depicts God hearing and speaking, loving and hating, and creating and destroying. Such language suggests that God is a mindful, conscious reality and thus personal or person-like.[48] We believe that Murdoch is on firmer ground than Davies. She describes the relationship between Anselm and God in terms of the reciprocal love between persons. "For Anselm, to think of God and to love him were one and the same" (1993: 440).[49]

Elucidating divine necessity: Murdoch recognized that in Anselmian Christianity, God is greater than that which cannot be conceived *(aliquid quo malus nihil cogitari potest)*. God is the maximally excellent, greatest possible being, what a later philosopher described as the most real being *(ens realissimum)*. God exists *a se* (self-sufficiently) and not *per alio* (through something else, like a wave, which is a mode or shape of something deeper, water).

Most commentators on Murdoch's treatment of Anselm's argument see her work as an occasion for making her case for the reality, indeed the necessity, of goodness in human life. As such, it has been described as a secularization of a profoundly religious argument for the existence of a personal God.

Murdoch brought her reading of Anselm's argument to bear on her view of the necessity of goodness and the Good. Murdoch's confidence in the necessity of goodness and the Good is illustrated by her thought experiment involving space visitors:

> If space visitors tell us that there is no value on their planet, this is not like saying there are no material objects. We would ceaselessly *look* for value in their society, wondering if they were lying, had different values, had misunderstood. (1993: 427)

Murdoch reinforced the previous point when she claimed that "we can 'think away' material objects from human existence, but not the concepts of good, true, and real" (1993: 425). Evidently, Murdoch's certainty in her moral realism is greater than her confidence that there is a material world. Putting this differently, it seems that Murdoch is convinced about the good,

---

[47] Anselm, *Proslogion II*, 101.
[48] Wolterstorff, *Divine Discourse*.
[49] In light of Davies' multiple publications opposing what he calls "personal theism," we do not think Murdoch and Davies merely have a difference in terminology.

true, and real, whether or not some form of idealism (that denies there are mind-independent material objects) was philosophically established.

Murdoch's claims about the necessity of the Good are forceful and help elucidate the difference between conditional and unconditional necessity. The necessity of Murdoch's Good is conditional. Given the reality of human life (and perhaps the life of space travelers), the absence of values and the Good is impossible. But human persons and, indeed, our whole cosmos are contingent. This stands in contrast to Anselm's notion of divine necessity, an unconditional necessity. If God exists, God exists as an unconditional necessity.

Murdoch on the use of religious experience in Anselm's argument: Murdoch proposed that Anselm's understanding of God "emerges from a context of deep belief and disciplined spirituality" (1993: 392). "Anselm's passionate certainty springs from his personal communion with God" (1993: 398). She wrote about Anselm's metaphysical reasoning being shaped by an appeal to experience:

> We are in the process of transition here to what may be seen as another and supplementary argument, a metaphysical argument which is also an appeal to experience. Of course good metaphysical arguments are successful appeals to experience, and can be seen too, as this one can, as aspects of other arguments which cluster round in support. Anselm makes the transition with natural ease. God is something necessary, not contingent.... How do we know about him then, and from whence do we derive the unique idea of good which can be extended into a concept of perfection? ... God, who is invisible and not an object in this world, can be seen and clearly seen everywhere in the visible things of the world, which are his creatures and his shadows. (1993: 395–396)

We interpret these and other remarks as suggesting that, according to Murdoch, at least some of the justification for Anselm's reasoning is that he has appeared to be in God's presence *(Coram Deo)*.[50] So, he has appeared to be in the presence of the greatest possible being; a reality greater than that cannot be conceived. If the being appears to be real, it certainly appears to be possible (*si res vera est, fieri potest:* if something is real, it is possible). His love of God is bound up with his experiencing a being whose nonexistence appears to be impossible. In Anselm's love for

---

[50] Although Murdoch does not cite him, Nicholas Rescher proposed a similar approach to the ontological argument as grounded in religious experience in "The Ontological Argument Revisited."

God, he finds a knowledge of God's reality (*amor ipse notitia est;* love is itself knowledge).[51]

Today, there is significant, positive philosophical work on the evidential significance of religious experience. See, for example, Kai-Man Kwan in his excellent book *The Rainbow of Experiences: A Defense of Holistic Empiricism*.

If we cast Anselm's reasoning in the context of religious experience, how effective is the argument? If you, like Murdoch, have lacked Anselm's experience of God, the reasoning will have no force, unless you accept the testimony of others to experience God on trust. But for those who have the requisite religious experiences, the argument may be as respectful as Descartes' "I think, therefore I am." Arguably, if you, reader, are justified in accepting that it is true that you are thinking, you are justified in thinking that you exist. Murdoch compares the Anselmian conclusion that God exists from his experience to the *cogito*: "In learning, loving, creatively imagining, we may be inspired or overcome by a sense of certainty at a particular point. (Compare the intuitive leap in Descartes' Proof.)" (1993: 400)

Murdoch does not see Anselm's reasoning as an instance of begging the question, but as a case of introducing the concept of God as revealed in experience and drawing out its implications (1993: 396). Murdoch thinks this is no more odd or peculiar than our own inquiry into values. We may begin with our intuitions, faith, or intuitive knowledge that, for example, we value and love persons, but we then gradually refine and justify these intuitions through reflection and experience. Here, then, is a Murdoch-inspired claim: If, based on his ostensible experience of *Coram Deo*, being in the presence of God, Anselm is justified in thinking it is possible that God – as a necessarily existing being – exists, then he is justified in thinking God's existence is not impossible and, therefore, necessary.

Does our Murdoch-inspired interpretation of Anselm's ontological argument lead to chaos? Could the appeal to cognitive appearings justify contradictory outcomes? Let us return to the case of the Tibetan story cited in Section 3. While Murdoch does not explicitly make this claim, a plausible interpretation of the mother venerating what she thinks is the relic of a Buddhist saint is that her experience of it seeming to glow "with miraculous light" (1993: 458) justified her trusting that the relic was authentic. Or,

---

[51] Gregory the Great, cited by Cottingham, 2006, 12. Anselm appears to be in the Augustinian tradition in which the awareness of God emerges through a longing or God's loving presence, especially as developed in the *Confessions*.

more modestly, that her veneration of the object (actually a dog's tooth) became an occasion for enlightenment or even, as some Buddhists believe, for the Buddha to appear to her.

We ourselves have a capacious view of justification and are not shocked by the idea that experiences may justify belief in different religions. In any case, we think the appeal to experience here is not anti-philosophical, and that the "job" of philosophers of religion is to consider such experiences along with a host of other factors (Is the Buddhist view of the self coherent? Is theism supported or undermined by independent arguments? And so on). Rarely is the case for a comprehensive worldview, such as Christianity, Buddhism, or secular naturalism, a matter of a single argument.

What about those who claim to experience God's nonexistence? Do they have evidence that God does not exist? The issue is complex. Some experiences of the absence of God may suggest that one is missing what was once present. For instance, one may feel abandoned or no longer loved by God. Perhaps some experiences can warrant atheism. Imagine the smartest professors and your peers are atheists and have what you think are compelling reasons for thinking God's existence is impossible. Imagine too you have never had anything that you might remotely describe as an experience of God or some good, transcendent being. Under those conditions, your atheism may be justified. Of course, an Anselmian theist might use the same reply, which we will consider later when Murdoch defends her view of the ubiquity of the good, notwithstanding those whose lives are destitute and seem pointless. Perhaps this should not overwhelm or undermine those who do experience goodness and the Good. Also, Murdoch maintains that both an Anselmian experience of God and the experience of the Good may take a great deal of intentionality, meditation, unselfing, and attention. In *Sartre: Romantic Rationalist*, Murdoch suggested that two philosophers, a Christian and a non-Christian, may look at the same world and yet, on "a personal plane," feel justified in reaching opposite conclusions (1987: 63). Murdoch wrote:

> The Christian philosopher Marcel broods upon the tenacity and reality of human communion in the midst of its obscurities and perversions. Here, by contrast Sartre shows us a non-Christian thinker. The individual is the centre, but a solipsistic centre. He has a *dream* of human companionship, but never the experience. He touches others at the fingertips. The best he can attain is an intuition of paradise, *un drole d'amitié* [a strange friendship]. (1987: 63)

Murdoch's point may apply here: A person who experiences what she takes to be the presence of God from a Christian point of view may be personally justified or warranted, notwithstanding the failure to recognize this from a Sartrean atheist perspective. Interestingly, in this example, Murdoch sides with the Christian perspective of Marcel rather than Sartre's.

Murdoch on standard objections to the argument: We agree with Murdoch that some common objections to Anselm's argument fail. Kant objected that the argument requires us to think of "existence" as a property. According to Kant, the property of existence adds nothing to the concept of a thing; for example, you don't add anything to the concept of a cat by changing the concept to an existing cat. Whatever Kant was thinking, the Anselmian seems to be coherent in treating *existing necessarily* as a conceivable property and a substantial one. Kant lacked that property or he would still be with us (as well as always existed). An early critic thought Anselm's argument might lead to absurdities like believing that a perfect island exists. But the concept of a perfect island has seemed as odd as imagining there could be a greatest possible number, unimaginable. Islands (like wizards, unicorns, and so on) are contingent. We fully agree with Murdoch that John Findlay fails in his attempt to turn the ontological argument into an argument that God cannot exist. Findlay simply assumes and provides us with no reason to think that only contingent beings can exist (1993: 411–412). If we knew that only contingent beings can exist, we would know there cannot be a necessarily existing being, but we don't know this.

To recapitulate: We suggest that Murdoch lays the foundation for reconstructing an Anselmian argument as follows: People may have experiences that they reasonably understand to be of God as maximally excellent. Murdoch does not express doubt that Anselm felt himself to be in communion with God. We can interpret Murdoch here, not committing herself to the existence of a personal God, but acknowledging that Anselm and those like him have what appears to them to be *bona fide* experiences of God. These experiences may be reasonably understood by Anselm and those like him to be of a being who exists unconditionally or necessarily. Because this *ipso facto* is the experience of a being who is deemed to be possible, such a person may reasonably believe that this being is not impossible or merely possible (an imaginary being), but necessarily exists in reality.

We put to one side historical matters of interpretation in terms of Anselm's actual argument(s). It will seem to most historians of the Murdoch-inspired argument as deflationary, aligning the ontological argument with theistic argument from experience. Be that as it may, we think the reconstructed argument is plausible. We surmise that Murdoch herself would not accept Anselmian theism, partly because she had not had the relevant religious experiences, but also because she raises two objections to Anselmian theism. Her first objection draws on her critique of structuralism and the second involves her view that the consoling figure of God and Christ may be fantasy and inferior to Buddha. We consider these two objections and, to be thorough, consider two further objections Murdoch raised.

Murdoch's first objection: Her objection is directed to a defender of Anselm's argument, Norman Malcolm. Malcolm defended the reasonability of believing that it is possible that God exists on the grounds that this is widely supported by many who believe (or report believing) they recognize God's abundant, maximal reality experientially. So, Malcolm wrote:

> At a deeper level, I suspect that the argument can be thoroughly understood by one who has a view of that human 'form of life' that gives rise to the idea of an infinitely great being, who views it from the inside not just in the outside and who has, therefore, at least some inclination to partake in that religious form of life. This inclination, in Kierkegaard's words, is 'from the emotions.'[52]

Malcolm elaborated on some of the relevant emotions, especially guilt and consolation. There is a great deal of evidence based on autobiography, liturgy, and religious practices of confession and absolution that millions of Christians have confessed sins before God and felt (or appeared to feel) absolved and loved by God.

Malcolm did not make this appeal as a proof that God's necessary existence is coherent, but as prima facie evidence that it is possible. "Prima facie" refers to a presumption of being evident that can, on reflection, be overturned.

Malcolm's approach seems sensible to us. That many people recognize what they take to be the reality of God is a reason for them to believe that God's existence is possible. Such a reason may be defeated by independent philosophical reasoning, but absent such reasoning, there is justification for the belief. If we have reason to believe that the concept of God is absurd, it would not matter how many billions of people believe in it. In the spirit of Malcolm's stance, we think that the failure of any philosopher to demonstrate that the idea of God as necessarily existing is incoherent, and the fact that billions of people find the idea of God coherent (including

---

[52] Malcolm, "Anselm's Ontological Arguments," 62.

some atheist philosophers who think that theism is coherent, but false) is evidence that Anselmian theism is coherent.[53]

Murdoch objected to Malcolm's defense on the grounds that it would lead to structuralism and various Wittgensteinian ills, like reintroducing the fact/value distinction, and possibly even move us toward emotivism in ethics. Malcolm's defense of the ontological argument used Wittgenstein's notion of a "form of life," which refers to a social-cultural setting in which language and meaning operate. Perhaps Murdoch surmised that appeals to different forms of life would usher in a social relativity that would undermine her moral realism.

We believe Murdoch's worries are misguided. Malcolm is simply pointing out that the God of Anselmian theism is widely, often lovingly attended to, and ostensibly real in the experience of countless people. For all we know, Malcolm may have had just as much antipathy to structuralism as Murdoch did. If Murdoch's commitment to moral realism would not be shaken by space travelers reporting that they had a form of life with no values (as cited earlier), why worry about Malcolm's referring to a form of life on our planet that has flourished for 2,000 years (among billions of Christians)? In fact, Murdoch's own appeal to the ordinary way in which people recognize values may be interpreted as her appealing to a form of life.[54]

Murdoch's second objection: Murdoch raised the following worries about the personal nature of Anselm's God:

> 'God' is the name of a supernatural person ... the really existing elsewhere, father figure. It makes a difference whether we believe in such a person, as it makes a difference whether Christ rose from the dead.... Perhaps (I believe) Christianity can continue without a personal God or a risen Christ, without belief in supernatural places and happenings, such as heaven, and life after death, but retaining the mystical figure of Christ occupying a place analogous to that of Buddha – a Christ who can console and save, but who is to be found as a living force within each human soul and not in some supernatural elsewhere.... The attractive figure of Christ appears in Christianity as a mediator, but might in some respects be an idol or barrier. (1993: 419–421)

So, Murdoch thought that Anselm's traditional Christianity may have some dispensable dangers: a father and son, Christ, who may be idols

---

[53] Copan and Taliaferro (eds.), *The Naturalness of Belief*. Taliaferro has defended a key epistemic principle in the ontological argument involving the use of conceivability to identify what is possible in "Sensibilia and Possibilia." Hartshorne defends Malcolm's main thesis that Murdoch objects to in Hartshorne 1965: 119.

[54] Actually, there has been a shift in anthropology in recent decades; there is now great stress on the widespread recognition of common values across cultures (or, if you will, different so-called forms of life); see Spencer Case, 2024: 78–83.

or projections, and false consoling fantasies, such as the beliefs in supernatural worlds like heaven.

Four brief replies:

First, the charge or worry about wish fulfilment works both ways. Some philosophers hope there is no God. And some wish that agnosticism is justified. The mere worry about being prey to wish fulfillment is unavoidable.

Second, Anselm's God is omnipresent, not "existing elsewhere." According to traditional theism, there is no place where God is not. There is no "elsewhere" when it comes to Anselmian theism.

Third, most forms of Buddhism conceive of an afterlife, a heaven and a hell. And many Buddhists believe Buddha is more than a force within us. Some hold that Buddha is omniscient.

Fourth, Christian theistic tradition has a richness and diversity that Murdoch may be underestimating. Christ would be a religious idol or barrier to God (or the Good) if some Unitarian theism is assumed. From the standpoint of Judaism, there can be no incarnation, and Islam celebrates Jesus as (only) a great prophet, only surpassed by Mohammad, and not God incarnate. But if traditional Christianity is true, Jesus is anything but an idol or barrier. Jesus is fully God and fully human and provides a way to find communion with God. Mulhall aptly observes how belief in the incarnation would vindicate (or lend support for) Murdoch's vision of the ubiquity of goodness:

> What matters primarily about the incarnation is what it tells us about God. For the idea that God might become fully human without any loss to His divinity, is before anything else, a way of articulating the conviction that not only human reality but reality as such is not essentially distant from that of God: it says not only that God loves His creation but that His creation – flesh and blood, time and history, life and death – is essentially consonant with, even expressive of, His own nature. And by denying that material creation is separated from the absolutely good by any abyss of essence, the Incarnation amounts to an endorsement of the realm of reality, a conviction of its essential value or goodness.[55]

If Mulhall is right, an incarnational Christianity would not hinder, but amplify Murdoch's view of goodness and the Good.

For the sake of ensuring that we have covered all (or most) of Murdoch's opposition to Anselmian theism, consider two further qualms: anthropomorphism and superstition.

On anthropomorphism, perhaps Murdoch was influenced by contemporaries like Oxford philosopher Anthony Kenny, who proposed that

---

[55] Mulhall, 'All the World Must Be "Religious"': Iris Murdoch's Ontological Arguments, 32.

the language used to describe God has meaning when applied to human or other embodied persons, but falls apart when used to describe an incorporeal being. In terms of the explanatory power of theism, perhaps Murdoch thought that the very category of the supernatural was the equivalent of something being superstitious or occult.

Anthropomorphism involves projecting human attributes when this is either unfitting or unjustified. Picturing God in human form (a bearded king) may be anthropomorphic, but it would seem too human-centric to suppose that thought and action and other person-like properties are exclusive to human beings. Shouldn't we be open to the possibility of personal, intelligent life in nonhuman forms (be it nonhuman animals or extraterrestrials, angels, demons, God, or what have you)? If we think that a dolphin is a thinking, feeling, reasoning animal, it is not clear that we are being anthropomorphic. Even if we go so far as to claim that a dolphin is a person, we are not thereby claiming a dolphin is a human.

As for superstition, it is evident that Murdoch did not embrace a strict, causal closure principle that requires scientific or philosophical determinism. She provided no a priori reason why the multiple reports of experiencing God as a transcendent, yet immanent reality should be universally rejected as spurious.[56] Her claim in *The Sovereignty of Good* that any sense of unity to human life "must be sought within human experience which has nothing outside it" is curious (1970: 77). We suggest that if we take her claim strictly or narrowly, it conflicts with her claims that we experience many things and events independent, "outside," us that are meaningful and valuable. And given the widespread reports of humans experiencing or perceiving God, we don't see how her dictum to restrict her purview to human experience would *ipso facto* rule out such reports. Murdoch is clearly well aware that philosophers (like Anselm, Augustine, and Julian of Norwich) make an appeal to experience that implicitly includes an experience of God (1993: 402). And while obviously Murdoch was not a Platonist with respect to forms, states of affairs, or mathematics, many historical and contemporary Platonists hold that on an everyday basis we reflect on, think about, and have a host of intentional relations – like love, desire, hate, hope, and fear – directed upon abstract or Platonic objects that exist independent of us.[57]

So, we ask, is her rejection of theism compelling? For the earlier reasons, we propose that, at the least, Murdoch has not given compelling reasons why someone who has had apparent experiences of the Anselmian God should treat those experiences as spurious or illusory.

---

[56] Taliaferro and Evans, *Is God Invisible?*
[57] Chisholm, *Person and Object.*

We end this section with different questions: Would a follower of Murdoch's central philosophical positions find a version of theism a plausible way to ground Murdoch's values? Is there a promising atheistic alternative that would enhance her values? In short, is it reasonable to claim, as Murdoch does in *The Sovereignty of Good:* "Our destiny can be examined but it cannot be justified or totally explained. We are simply here" (1970: 77)? The word "cannot" is a stringent term, implying that *it is impossible for there to be a broader explanatory, luminous perspective.* We are not persuaded she has demonstrated this impossibility.

5.3 Platonic Accounts of Why We Are Here

We suggest that there are multiple, broad metaphysical frameworks that can ground and enhance Murdochian values. We sketch only two that appeal to a necessary, essentially good reality: One is nontheistic (or atheistic), and the other is theistic. As noted earlier, we think such frameworks may offer a broader, ultimate framework and yet not totally justify and explain *everything.* Both accounts that follow may allow that there are chance (random) events and undetermined free choices.

An appealing nontheistic framework for a Murdochian to consider is that our cosmos exists due to a good, necessarily existing, impersonal, but purposive force or element. According to what is known as axiarchism, values explain or rule the natural order. Things exist because they ought to exist. One version of axiarchism today is known as euteleological philosophical theology.[58] It denies there is a personal God, and yet retains the idea that our cosmos has an originative and sustaining cause and the conviction that this ultimate cause (perhaps the universe itself) is teleological, oriented to goodness or the Good. "Euteleological" is from the Greek "eu" meaning "good" or "well" and "teleological" is from "telos" or "purpose." Because this ultimate reality is not a person with divine attributes like omnipotence and omniscience, it would not offer loving providential care for all persons and all aspects of the cosmos, but it could still offer an account of why there is a cosmos. And it might even be used to provide some support for life after death for persons, if such an afterlife would be good. The goodness of life after death would seem worthy of consideration if you, like Murdoch, think that persons are inexhaustively valuable and that loving persons are at

---

[58] Bishop and Perszyk, *God, Purpose, and Reality*. For related views involving teleological or axiological explanations of the cosmos without personal agency, see Leslie, *Value and Existence* and Parfit, "The Puzzle of Reality" and Rice, *God and Goodness*.

the heart of morality. If it is possible for loving persons to continue after bodily death, why would that not be good? The British idealist J. M. E. McTaggart was an atheist who believed that after death we will form a community of loving souls. We suggest this might comport well with Murdoch's notion that our pilgrimages are developmental and not fully realized in this life. She said:

> The unity and fundamental reality of goodness is an image and support of the unity and fundamental reality of the individual. What is fundamental here is ideal or transcendent, never fully realized or analyzed, but continually rediscovered in the course of the daily struggle with the world, and the imagination and passion whereby it is carried on. (1993: 427)

Of course, if an afterlife is known to be metaphysically impossible, there is no point in hoping for one. But if it is possible and good, perhaps the euteleological force would have a purpose for death not to be the annihilation of persons, but a transition to a greater pilgrimage. Interestingly, philosopher Peter Geach – the husband of Elizabeth Anscombe, to whom Murdoch dedicated *Metaphysics as a Guide to Morals* – defended McTaggart's mystical vision of love after death. See Geach's *Truth, Love, and Immortality*. Two other famous twentieth-century philosophers who were atheists but held that an individual afterlife is possible were C. D. Broad and C. J. Ducasse.

Another option would be some form of theistic Platonism. Because of Murdoch's admiration for Christianity, consider Christian Platonism as developed by Clement and Origin of Alexandria, Augustine, Anselm, the Florentine Platonists, the Cambridge Platonists, and current representatives, as described in the book *Christian Platonism: A History* (Hampton and Kenney 2021). This form of Christianity gives a central role of the Good, the True, and the Beautiful in understanding God and creation. It recognizes the positive, loving dimensions of reality along with the debilitating horrors, while maintaining faith, hope, and love that the God who creates and sustains the cosmos will bring good out of evil.

The appeal of Christian Platonism becomes vivid near the end of Murdoch's *Metaphysics as a Guide to Morals* in the chapter "The Void." We cite Mulhall's account of that chapter, which refers to the philosopher whom Murdoch deeply admired: Simone Weil. Mulhall wrote:

> Drawing upon Weil, Murdoch here draws attention to experiences of absolute affliction, of pain and evil which occasion desolation: 'black misery, bereavement, remorse, frustrated talent, loneliness, humiliation,

depression, secret woe' ... And she asks, 'can we go on talking about a spiritual source and an absolute good if a majority of human kind is debarred from it?' The challenge is clear: if human beings can be placed in situations which strip or shatter the personality, which denude them of all energy and motivation, and render the world utterly charmless and without attraction, then it seems that it simply cannot be true that Good is always and everywhere magnetic, that loving attention to the world will attract us to a clearer image of reality, that our transformative energies are never entirely in abeyance.

Murdoch is naturally hesitant in her treatment of this fundamental counter-example to her moral vision. She reminds us that such episodes pass: but the key question here is not their permanence or frequency, but what they reveal about the nature of the real. She also points out that, according to Weil herself, the void can give spiritual succor, in so far as it teaches us that we are absolutely nothing, that we can lose everything we have and are; but she does not emphasize that Weil's ability to draw succor from such a teaching depends entirely upon her ability to locate the void within an essentially Christian framework of understanding.[59]

We think Mulhall's observations are important and illuminating.

The Christian Platonism of Weil can provide hope and faith in the ubiquity of the good because of the magnetic power of the all-loving, omnipotent God. Without God's overwhelming loving power, the void might have the last word.

We suggested earlier that an atheistic Platonism might include a good afterlife. It seems that Christian Platonism, with its recognition of a God who loves persons, would have reasons for ensuring that creatures not perish at death, but find redemption in a life beyond life.

While a Murdochian might still bristle about thinking of God in personal terms, there is this to consider: If you follow Murdoch in thinking that persons and personhood are great goods, why would one not hope to find personhood realized in its highest form possible, the *ens realissimum* (the most real being)?

So, we end our pilgrimage with you through Murdoch's philosophical work with questions for further inquiry. But we also end by commending her work to you without reservation; we have no questions about the breadth, depth, integrity, creativity, and protean mind of Dame Iris Murdoch.

---

[59] Mulhall, 'All the World Must Be "Religious"': Iris Murdoch's Ontological Arguments, 33.

Bibliography

Adams, M. (2000). *Horrendous Evils and the Goodness of God*. Ithaca: Cornell University Press.

Alston, W. (1993). *Perceiving God: The Epistemology of Religious Experience*. Ithaca: Cornell University Press.

Anscombe, G. E. M. (1981, [1975]). The First Person. In The Collected Philosophical Papers of G. E. M. Anscombe, vol. 2, *Metaphysics and Philosophy of Mind*. Oxford: Blackwell, 21–36.

Anselm of Canterbury. (2008). In B. Davies and G. R. Evans, eds., *The Major Works*. Oxford: Oxford University Press.

Bayley, J. (1989). Foreword. In P. J. Conradi, ed., *The Saint and the Artist: A Study of the Fiction of Iris Murdoch*. San Francisco: HarperCollins, xi–xii.

Bishop, J. and K. Perszyk. (2023). *God, Purpose, and Reality*. Oxford: Oxford University Press.

Bolton, L. (2023). Murdoch and Feminism. In S. C. Caprioglio and M. Hopwood, eds., *The Murdochian Mind*. London: Routledge, 438–450.

Bradley, F. H. (1969, [1893]). *Appearance and Reality*. London: Allen & Unwin.

Case, Stanley. (2024). *Is Morality Real? A Debate*. London: Routledge.

Cavell, Stanley. (2015). *Must We Mean What We Say?* Cambridge: Cambridge University Press.

Chisholm, R. (1976). *Person and Object*. LaSalle: Open Court.

Clarke, Bridget. (2018). Murdoch. In S. Leach and J. Tartaglia, eds., *The Meaning of Life and the Great Philosophers*. London: Routledge.

Conradi, P. J. (2001). *Iris Murdoch: A Life*. San Francisco: HarperCollins.

Conradi, P. J. (2001). *The Saint and the Artist: A Study of the Fiction of Iris Murdoch*. San Francisco: HarperCollins.

Copan, P. and C. Taliaferro, eds. (2019). *The Naturalness of Belief: New Essays on Theism's Rationality*. New York: Lexington Press.

Cottingham, J. (2006). *The Spiritual Dimension*. Cambridge: Cambridge University Press.

Cumhaill, C. M. and R. Wiseman. (2023). *Metaphysical Animals: How Four Women Brought Philosophy Back to Life*. New York: Anchor Books.

Davies, B. (2010). Simplicity. In C. Meister and C. Taliaferro, eds., *Christian Philosophical Theology*. Cambridge: Cambridge University Press, 31–45.

Dooley, G., ed. (2003). *From a Tiny Corner in the House of Fiction: Conversations with Iris Murdoch*. Columbia: University of South Carolina Press.

Geach, P. (1979). *Truth, Love, and Immortality: An Introduction to McTaggart's Philosophy*. Los Angeles: University of California Press.

Gerson, L. P. (2020). *Platonism and Naturalism*. Ithaca: Cornell University Press.

Hampshire, S. (1981, [1959]). *Thought and Action*. Notre Dame: University of Notre Dame Press.

Hampton, A. and J. P. Kenney, eds. (2021). *Christian Platonism: A History*. Cambridge: Cambridge University Press.

Harper, R. (1955). *Sleeping Beauty and Other Essays*. Cambridge: Cowley Press.

Hartshorne, Charles. (1965). *Anselm's Discovery*. LaSalle: Open Court.

Hawkins, P. (2019). Iris Murdoch: Atheist, but Unapologetically Anglican. *Church Times*, 19 July. www.churchtimes.co.uk/articles/2019/19-july/features/features/

Jacobs, A. (1995). G(o)od in Iris Murdoch. *First Things*, 1 February. www.firstthings.com/good-in-iris-murdoch/

Kwan, K. M. (2011). *The Rainbow of Experiences, Critical Trust, and God: A Defense of Holistic Empiricism*. London: Continuum.

Leftow, B. (2022). *Anselm's Argument: Divine Necessity*. Oxford: Oxford University Press.

Leslie, J. (1979). *Value and Existence*. Oxford: Blackwell.

Lewis, H. D. (1969). *The Elusive Mind*. London: George Allen & Unwin.

Lipscomb, B. J. B. (2021). *The Women Are Up to Something: How Elizabeth Anscombe, Philippa Foot, Mary Midgley, and Iris Murdoch Revolutionized Ethics*. Oxford: Oxford University Press.

Loose, J. et al., eds. (2018). *The Blackwell Companion to Substance Dualism*. Oxford: Wiley-Blackwell.

Malcolm, N. (1960). Anselm's Ontological Arguments. *Philosophical Review*, 69, 41–62.

Midgley, M. (2013). The Golden Age of Female Philosophy. *The Guardian*, 28 November.

Moore, G. E. (1903). The Refutation of Idealism. *Mind*, 12(48), 433–453.

Mothersill, M. (1987). *Beauty Restored*. Oxford: Oxford University Press.

Mulhall, S. (2007). All the World Must Be "Religious": Iris Murdoch's Ontological Arguments. In A. Rowe, ed., *Iris Murdoch: A Reassessment*. New York: Palgrave.

Murdoch, I. (1968). Interview with W. K. Rose. *London Magazine*, Winter, 3–22.
Murdoch, I. (1970). *The Sovereignty of Good*. London: Routledge.
Murdoch, I. (1976). *A Severed Head*. London: Penguin.
Murdoch, I. (1987 [1953]). *Sartre: Romantic Rationalist*. London: Penguin.
Murdoch, I. (1993 [1992]). *Metaphysics as a Guide to Morals*. London: Penguin.
Murdoch, I. (1997). *Existentialists and Mystics: Writings on Philosophy and Literature*. In P. Conradi, ed. London: Penguin.
Murdoch, I. (2001). *The Sea, The Sea*. London: Penguin.
Murdoch, I. (2011). *Iris Murdoch, a Writer at War: Letters and Diaries 1939–1945*. P. Conradi, ed. Oxford: Oxford University Press.
Nachmanovitch, S. (1990). *Free Play: Improvisation in Life and Art*. New York: G. P. Putnam's Sons.
Nagasawa, Y. (2017). *Maximal God: A New Defense of Perfect Being Theism*. Oxford: Oxford University Press.
Nagel, T. (1974). What Is It Like to Be a Bat? *Philosophical Review*, 83(4), 435–450.
Nussbaum, M. (1996). Love and Vision: Iris Murdoch on Eros and the Individual. In M. Antonaccio and W. Schweiker, eds., *Iris Murdoch and the Search for Human Goodness*. Chicago: University of Chicago Press, 29–53.
Parfit, D. (1992). The Puzzle of Reality: Why Does the Universe Exist? *Times Literary Supplement*, 3 July.
Passmore, J. (1951). The Dreariness of Aesthetics. *Mind*, 60(239), 318–335.
Pears, D. (1988). *The False Prison: The Development of Wittgenstein's Philosophy*. Oxford: Clarendon.
Plato. (1994). Republic. In E. Hamilton and H. Cairns, eds., *The Collected Dialogues of Plato*. Translated by Paul Shorey. Princeton: Princeton University Press.
Rice, H. (2000). *God and Goodness*. Oxford: Oxford University Press.
Robjant, D. (2011). As a Buddhist Christian; the Misappropriation of Iris Murdoch. *Heythrop Journal*, 52(6), 993–1008.
Rose, W. K. (1968). Iris Murdoch, Informally, interview, *London Magazine*, 8(3): 59–73. In G. Dooley (ed.), (2003), *From a Tiny Corner in the House of Fiction: Conversations with Iris Murdoch*. Columbia: University of South Carolina Press, 16–29.
Rudd, A. (2022). *Painting and Presence: Why Paintings Matter*. Oxford: Oxford University Press.

Ryle, G. (2002 [1949]). *The Concept of Mind*. Chicago: Chicago University Press.

Sacks, O. (1999 [1973]). *Awakenings*. New York: Vintage Press.

Sacks, O. (2021). *The Man Who Mistook His Wife for a Hat*. New York: Vintage Books.

Sartre, J. P. (1993 [1943]). *Being and Nothingness*. Translated by H. E. Barnes. New York: Washington Square Press.

Sartre, J. P. (2013 [1938]). *Nausea*. Translated by L. Alexander. New York: New Directions.

Steiner, George. (1997). Foreword. *Existentialists and Mystics*.

Strawson, Galen. (1994). *Mental Reality*. Cambridge: Massachusetts Institute of Technology Press.

Taliaferro, C. (2001). Sensibility and Possibilia. *Philosophia Christi*, 3(2), 403–420.

Taliaferro, C. (2005). *Evidence and Faith: Philosophy and Religion since the Seventeenth Century*. Cambridge: Cambridge University Press.

Taliaferro, C. (2021). *Religions: A Quick Immersion*. New York: Tibidabo Press.

Taliaferro, C. and J. Evans. (2013). *The Image in Mind: Theism, Naturalism, and the Imagination*. London: Bloomsbury.

Taliaferro, C. and J. Evans. (2021). *Is God Invisible? An Essay on Religion and Aesthetics*. Cambridge: Cambridge University Press.

Van Inwagen, P, (2014). *Existence: Essays in Ontology*. Cambridge: Cambridge University Press.

Weil, S. (2001). *The Need for Roots*. London: Routledge.

Wittgenstein, L. (1953). *Philosophical Investigations*. Translated by G. M. E. Anscombe. London: Pearson.

Wolterstorff, N. (1995). *Divine Discourse: Philosophical Reflections on the Claim that God Speaks*. Cambridge: Cambridge University Press.

Acknowledgments

We thank Alexander J. B. Hampton for his support of this work. We are grateful to two anonymous reviewers of our proposal as well as grateful for the two reviewers of the completed manuscript. We thank Kathleen Weflen for her expert editing and advice. We are grateful to Rebecca Judge and Anthony Becker for their generous support of our project. We thank Ben Glaros for introducing us to the work of Stephen Nachmanovitch.

Cambridge Elements

History of Philosophy and Theology in the West

Alexander J. B. Hampton
University of Toronto

Alexander J. B. Hampton is a professor at the University of Toronto, specialising in metaphysics, poetics, and nature. His publications include *Romanticism and the Re-Invention of Modern Religion* (Cambridge 2019), *Christian Platonism: A History* (ed.) (Cambridge, 2021), and the *Cambridge Companion to Christianity and the Environment* (ed.) (Cambridge, 2022).

Editorial Board

Shaun Blanchard, *University of Notre Dame, Australia*
Jennifer Newsome Martin, *University of Notre Dame, USA*
Sean McGrath, *Memorial University*
Willemien Otten, *University of Chicago*
Catherine Pickstock, *University of Cambridge*
Jacob H. Sherman, *California Institute of Integral Studies*
Charles Taliaferro, *St. Olaf College*

About the Series

In the history of philosophy and theology, many figures and topics are considered in isolation from each other. This series aims to complicate this binary opposition, while covering the history of this complex conversation from antiquity to the present. It reconceptualizes traditional elements of the field, generating new and productive areas of historical enquiry, and advancing creative proposals based upon the recovery of these resources.

Cambridge Elements

History of Philosophy and Theology in the West

Elements in the Series

The Metaphysics of Divine Participation
Alexander J. B. Hampton

C. S. Lewis on the Soul, God, and Christianity
Stewart Goetz

Popper, Philosophy and Faith
Anthony O'Hear

Leo XIII and the Rise of Neo-Thomism
Valfredo Maria Rossi

A Critical Genealogy of Humanism
Friedemann Stengel

Augustine and the Natural Law
Katherine Chambers

Iris Murdoch and the Transcendent
Charles Taliaferro and Jil Evans

A full series listing is available at: www.cambridge.org/EHPT

For EU product safety concerns, contact us at Calle de José Abascal, 56–1°, 28003 Madrid, Spain or eugpsr@cambridge.org.

www.ingramcontent.com/pod-product-compliance
Lightning Source LLC
LaVergne TN
LVHW011855060526
838200LV00054B/4347